The New

SCI FI

TV

James Van Hise

PIONEER BOOKS INC

Recently Released Pioneer Books. . .

TO ORDER CALL TOLL FREE: (800)444-2524 ext. 67
credit cards happily accepted

Library of Congress Cataloging-in-Publication Data
James Van Hise, 1959—

    The New SCI FI TV

    1. The New SCI FI TV
(television, popular culture)
I. Title

Published by Pioneer Books, Inc., 5715 N. Balsam Rd., Las Vegas, NV, 89130.

PUBLISHER, EDITOR, DESIGNER: Hal Schuster   DESIGN INSPIRATION: Ben Long

Cover Photo ©1994 PARAMOUNT PICTURES

Table of Contents

The New

SCI FI

TV

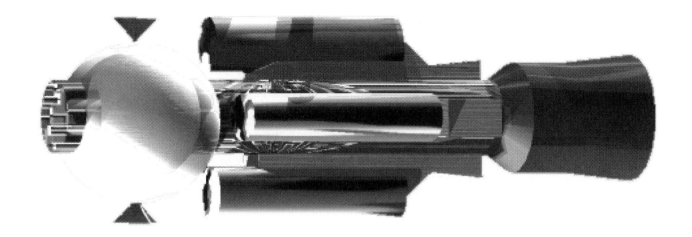

MODERN
SCIENCE FICTION TELEVISION

Science fiction television today has come a long way since BATTLESTAR: GALACTI-CA, BUCK ROGERS, and AUTOMAN. Those shows from the '70s and early '80s failed to understand what made STAR TREK successful. They tried to reinvent the wheel and delivered a rickety cube.

Current producers benefit from watching the rebirth of STAR TREK as both NEXT GENERATION and DEEP SPACE NINE. They realize characters and stories of human consequence drive a popular series.

THE X-FILES offers human beings with internal strengths and weaknesses confronting the unknown. HIGHLANDER's protagonist learns to live with immortality and his very human need to love and be loved. The cyborg ROBOCOP suffers from a fear of losing his humanity while the world crumbles around him.

SEAQUEST DSV delivers an optimistic view of the near future with a mammoth experimental submarine populated by people possessing very human concerns. LOIS & CLARK presents a romance between a man and a woman learning to fit into each other's lives.

BABYLON 5 challenges STAR TREK on its home ground with a space station populated by humans and aliens experiencing the ultimate culture clash. William Shatner's TEK-WAR features near future detective stories of humans in conflict with their technology.

TIME TRAX began with an interesting premise, telling nice little character stories. Unfortunately it repeated the same story too many times until it was canceled at the end of its second season.

Science fiction TV shows now offer a variety of worlds and types of stories. They flex their imagination muscles to deliver something new and interesting. So long as they keep trying to come up with things different from what came before there will be many more bright spots on the creative horizon.

—- JAMES VAN HISE
June, 1994

The Fox Network's sole science fiction entry has captured much audience interest. Viewers who don't watch science fiction other than STAR TREK tune in to this series.

THE X-FILES

Fans of fantastic television have found a new hour to savor each Friday night: THE X-FILES. The Fox Network took a big chance with THE X-FILES, but it's paid off. The high rated series has been renewed for a second season.

THE X-FILES is scary. It started with stories about UFOs, alien abductions and government cover-ups. FBI agents Fox Mulder and Dana Scully pursue special cases with mysterious elements and paranormal overtones, "X files."

Mulder is an expert in these areas, and appears obsessed with them. They earned him the nickname, "Spooky" Mulder. Other agents regard him as a nut case.

Partners don't stick with Mulder for long. He's certain his newest one, Dr. Dana Scully, was sent to evaluate whether he's wasting the FBI's time and money in his odd pursuits.

She turns out to be the perfect partner for him. In the premiere episode, "THE X-FILES," Scully gets an eyeful when a murder investigation in Oregon reveals a coffin containing a withered corpse. Series creator Chris Carter wrote and Robert Mandel directed the story.

A scene from a mysterious episode of THE X FILES.

High school classmates are being abducted and experimented on by aliens. Scully is skeptical despite bizarre evidence including an inexplicable metal object implanted in the nose of one of the corpses.

The case remains officially unresolved; the new team goes on to their next assignment. The premiere ends with a mysterious man carrying the device through an immense, top-secret government warehouse in the Pentagon and filing it with several more just like it!

SECRETS HIDDEN IN SECRET PLACES

This is a place Mulder would love to get into—the place where the government keeps its proof of the impossible. This will be a recurring theme in the show: Mulder looks for proof, Scully acts skeptical, and dark government agencies counter them at almost every turn.

The heroes may work for the government, but that government cannot be trusted. It enhances the paranoia of the series.

Executive producer/writer Chris Carter insists on a scientific attitude. The opening credits tell us the truth is out there, but the show never offers a supernatural explanation— only paranormal ones. THE X-FILES is the first show Carter pitched to Fox. They were wise to latch on to it, as it has survived its lead-in, THE ADVENTURES OF BRISCO COUNTY, JR.

Carter once worked on the editorial staff of SURFING magazine. He also wrote and produced numerous TV pilots and worked on Disney TV movies before taking this great leap into the unknown.

His favorite childhood television series was KOLCHAK: THE NIGHT STALKER. Carter realized his life's ambition by creating a truly scary show. THE X-FILES has already run twice as many episodes as its 1970s' predecessor. Fans of THE X-FILES want Mulder's father to appear on the show played by Kolchak's Darren McGavin!

WHO IS FOX MULDER?

Carter began by carefully crafting the man who would lead viewers into the darker realms of scientific possibility, Agent Fox Mulder. An Oxford-trained psychologist, Mulder is one of the FBI Violent Crimes division's best agents. He has tracked down a number of serial killers.

Along the way, Mulder came across the 'X' files shunted aside by the Bureau. They became his obsession, on duty and off. Viewers soon learn the source of Mulder's fascination for the inexplicable.

When the twelve-year old Mulder lived in Chilmark, Massachusetts, his eight-year old sister disappeared. He thinks she was abducted by aliens.

Gillian Anderson and David Duchovny of THE X FILES. **Photo ©1994 Fox Broadcasting Co.**

Under hypnotic regression he recalled a bright light that rendered him immobile while she was taken away. A voice told him she would be all right.

Scully learns of this in the fourth episode, "Conduit." She is no more convinced of the existence of UFOs than before, but understands Mulder better.

Carter hired David Duchovny to bring Mulder to life. A veteran of WORKING GIRL, THE RAPTURE, and KALIFORNIA, the actor is best known as the transvestite FBI agent in three second-season episodes of David Lynch's TWIN PEAKS TV series. Duchovny embarked on his acting career after opting out of the doctoral program in English literature at Yale.

He didn't think THE X-FILES would last on television because it would focus on UFOs. Its variety proved to be its strong point, but viewers are intrigued by episodes furthering the mystery of Fox Mulder's connection with UFOs.

Duchovny makes Mulder human. This isn't easy with a character distracted to the point of catalepsy, but Mulder adds a unique sense of humor every week in a perfect deadpan delivery.

MORE THAN JUST AN ASSISTANT

The other hero is Dana Scully, a medical doctor with an undergraduate degree in physics. The FBI recruited her right out of medical school.

Scully taught at the FBI Academy in Quantico, Virginia until she was assigned as Mulder's partner. Section Chief Scott Blevins wants to keep an eye on him and his obsession with the X files.

Scully is skeptical of the paranormal. She believes everything has a logical, scientific explanation. Mulder agrees in principle, but the two agents don't see eye-to-eye as to what is scientifically possible. In most cases, Scully doesn't witness paranormal events.

Stage actress Gillian Anderson portrays Dana Scully as sexy and smart. The character thinks on her feet. She is open minded enough to respect Mulder despite her skepticism. It's doubtful the tension between the characters will lead to romance, but the possibility intrigues many viewers.

The second episode, "Deep Throat," continues the UFO theme. It introduces an important character, a high government official without a name, referred to by the series writers only as "Deep Throat." Actor Jerry Hardin makes "DT" a mysterious individual.

"DT" warns Mulder not to take an assignment, then helps him on the "Eden" case. He later provides classified information for Mulder's unauthorized investigation in "Fallen Angel." Scully knew nothing of him, but Mulder was able to contact him when needed.

In "Deep Throat," Mulder and Scully head to Ellens Air Force Base in Idaho. Their decision is opposed by very mysterious and powerful people. The disappearance of a test

Special agents Mulder and Scully (David Duchovny and Gillian Anderson) of THE X FILES

Photo ©1994 Fox Broadcasting Co.

pilot leads to the possibility that the US. Military has been experimenting on UFOs.

A WORLD FILLED WITH STRANGENESS

THE X-FILES is more than a show about UFOs. Mulder covers the entire paranormal waterfront.

"Squeeze" introduces an unnerving killer, a man who stretches his body into impossible shapes. The opening sequence provides a twist on the classic locked-room murder mystery.

A businessman is stalked to his office by a killer who enters through a small ventilation grate. The killing, involving the removal of the victim's liver, bears the trademark of a serial killer. Mulder links the case with earlier murders, in 1963 and 1933, and, possibly, even earlier crimes.

When Eugene Tooms is found hiding in the murder building, Mulder adds interesting questions to his lie detector test: "Is Tooms a hundred years old?" and

"Did he ever go to the city where the earlier killings took place?" Tooms' answers show he is lying.

The nature of the questions renders the answers useless to anyone but Mulder. He finds records of a Eugene Tooms born in 1903, but cannot locate any death records. The original murder occurred in the building in which Tooms then lived.

The FBI agents locate a cop from the 1933 case. The officer keeps a well-documented archive. He believes Eugene is a genetic mutation who must hibernate every 30 years, but only after collecting five human livers to sustain him.

Tooms tries to kill Scully and is captured and incarcerated— but only for his attack on Scully. No one can link him to his gruesome killings. When a guard brings food to his cell, he eyes the food slot and smiles.

SOMETHING IS OUT THERE

The show returned to UFO territory in "Conduit." The case of a vanished teenager recalls Mulder's memories of his sister's disappearance.

The mother of the missing girl was a well-known UFO contactee in her youth. Embittered by exposure and mockery after revealing her experience, she is determined to keep UFOs out of her daughter's case. Her young son seems to be receiving binary information through the static in their TV, writing down ones and zeros on countless sheets of paper.

When Mulder takes a page in for analysis, the National Security Agency steps in and ransacks the family's house. The boy has somehow written down top-secret satellite transmissions!

Mulder uncovers a semi-related murder, but hits a dead end. In one eerie scene, the boy covers the floor with sheets of paper, which, when viewed from the top of the stairs by Scully, turns out to be a binary representation of his missing sister's face.

An East Coast version of Sasquatch provides the mystery in "The Jersey Devil." The case opens when a cannibalized human body is found in New Jersey State Park. The local police are covering something up, making this Atlantic City investigation difficult for Mulder and Scully.

The "Devil" is a female in a frenzied state after the death of her mate. The humanoids, according to Mulder, are an evolutionary diversion that survived in the forest for ages.

SECRETS TO DIE FOR

Mulder and Scully then tackle a poltergeist in "Shadows." In a stunning opening sequence, a secretary whose boss recently committed suicide is attacked. Her assailants are killed by an unseen force with superhuman power.

Stakeout photos reveal her dead boss' ghostly face hovering near her. Her late boss had discovered his company providing crucial electronics to Middle-Eastern terrorists and threatened to blow the whistle. His suicide was really murder.

The secretary is a threat to the corrupt company head. Her boss protects her from beyond the grave. The episode ends when the vengeful spirit creates a whirlwind in a locked office and threatens the devil boss with a Cross pen!

As luck would have it, Scully is locked out of the office and doesn't witness any of this. Mulder talks the ghost into sparing the killer and revealing the hiding place of the incriminating evidence.

"Ghost in the Machine" is a dud. An elaborate computerized high-rise office security system develops a mind of its own, and a murderous streak. The government, this time in the form of the Defense Department, wants Mulder to stay out of the way so they can get their hands on this new weapon.

STRANGE DAYS FOR SURE

"Ice" threatens to turn into a carbon copy of John Carpenter's THE THING, but redeems itself with a truly paranoid scene. Mulder and Scully, and a few other personnel, are trapped in an Arctic research facility with an extraterrestrial blood parasite.

No one can trust anyone, especially after someone is found murdered. Mulder is locked in a closet when his weird views make everyone, including Scully, suspect him of having fallen prey to the virus. Of course, it turns out to be someone else. . . and they discover a cure, of sorts.

"Space" centers on space shuttle sabotage. Space program fan Mulder is happy to help a NASA worker who doesn't trust his project head, a former astronaut. The project head has never been the same since a disembodied entity passed through him on a space walk decades earlier.

Gillian Anderson as Agent Scully examines the X Files.   Photo ©1994 Fox Broadcasting Co.

'Deep Throat' alerts Mulder to a UFO crash site in "Fallen Angel." The military tries to keep Mulder away while bringing an extraterrestrial force into captivity. When he is discovered, Mulder's position in the FBI is jeopardized.

EVE OF DESTRUCTION

A death with all the neck marks of a vampire attack draws Mulder and Scully to Connecticut in "Eve." A duplicate murder is discovered in California at the same time. Deep Throat tells Mulder of a secret project to create a genetically engineered super race.

"Fire" begins with a case of spontaneous combustion. A British lord burst into flames, observed by his family and their gardener.

On the other side of the Atlantic, Mulder is contacted by Phoebe Green, a British woman he's known since school in England. His former lover now works for Scotland Yard and needs his help.

Members of Parliament have died in flames after their wives received anonymous love letters. She's been assigned to protect Lord Marsden on his visit to the States; his wife has received a letter.

Mulder is intrigued by the possibility that the killer is pyrokinetic. He is afraid of fire and this case may give him a chance to master the fear.

Dana Scully's father dies in "Beyond the Sea." He later appears sitting in a chair in her apartment. She chalks it up to stress, even though it occurred before she learned of his death.

Meanwhile, Mulder investigates a kidnapping. A death row inmate claims to have information. He says that ever since he received a reprieve while literally standing in the gas chamber he can commune with the dead. Mulder thinks the convict is a fake with a link to the kidnaper.

In a series twist, Scully believes the man because he says things only her father knew. Mulder tells her it can't be so.

The killer plays a mind game with Scully.

Sometimes he appears to be psychic. Other times he's obviously faking. With remarkable accuracy, he predicts a shoot-out in which Mulder is wounded.

Scully tells the killer he has a deal. He tells her to attend his execution to hear a final message from her father. His information rescues the kidnapped young couple, results in the death of the kidnapper, and saves Mulder's life.

It seems he was really psychic, at least some of the time. Scully decides not to attend the execution, where the killer sees a vision of the spirits of his victims, his own family, coming to carry him off. Brad Dourif delivers an excellent performance as the death row psychic.

WHO IS DEEP THROAT?

Mulder and Scully visit an Amish-type religious community in "Gender Bender." The murders prove difficult to solve when the serial killer appears to switch genders.

In "Lazarus" Scully almost believes the unbelievable after an old lover and fellow agent, Jack Willis, is shot on a bank stakeout. The foiled bank robber is killed, or so it seems. Actually his spirit took over the body of the wounded Willis in the emergency room.

Mulder catches on first. Scully resists until Mulder sends "Willis" a birthday card and "Willis" accepts it without comment. Mulder knows Willis and Scully shared the same birthday many months earlier.

Scully is abducted by "Willis" and held captive in the bank robber's girl-friend's home. Scully tries to bring the real Willis back, but he dies. The spirit that possessed him didn't know he was diabetic.

In "Young at Heart," Mulder is stalked by a killer he caught early in his career. The killer hasn't aged a day since!

With Scully's help, Mulder survives to take on a UFO case in "E.B.E." 'Deep Throat' briefs Mulder, and he takes Scully to Tennessee. The military has the contents of a UFO that crashed near Iraq.

UFO sightings follow the trail of the truck carrying the mysterious cargo. The heroes follow in close pursuit.

Deep Throat is revealed to be very powerful, but may be working against Mulder. The government's motives are very unclear.

MYSTERIES IN THE DEEP WOODS

In "Miracle Man," a young faith healer causes several deaths. Mulder, with Scully in tow, heads to the deep South to investigate. He thinks the boy has real psychic powers.

A dead Native American draws Mulder into "Shapes.". The man who shot him insists he killed an animal, and he may not be lying. Mulder believes there may be truth in Indian legends.

The agents head to the Pacific Northwest to investigate the disappearance of thirty loggers in "Darkness Falls." Anti-logging activists have been spiking trees and harassing loggers, and local law-enforcement suspects them of going too far.

There is also evidence the loggers were illegally cutting old growth trees. Looking at the stump of a recently cut ancient tree, Mulder and Scully spot the impossible. A ring deep inside the tree shows signs of recent life.

At night, bizarre swarming insects prove to be the real culprits. They were released from their dormant larval state when the tree was cut down.

Are they alien or merely some evolutionary fluke? There's little time to wonder. Mulder, Scully, and a few locals endure a night in a cabin besieged by bugs kept at bay only by the light from a generator low on gas.

The light gives out just after dawn. Fortunately, they find a working vehicle, and government clean-up teams rescue them. Later, in a top-security hospital, Mulder learns the government will contain this threat. They will destroy the entire forest if necessary.

BACK FROM THE PAST

An old adversary returns in "Tooms." The mutant Tooms was incarcerated because of his attack on Scully. No one pinned any murders on him.

He's been held in a psychiatric facility. Mulder tries to prevent his release, but instead appears crazy to the review board. Tooms is released into a foster home and resumes his old job with the Baltimore Animal Control Department.

Muller and Scully again turn to the cop who covered the case in the 1930s. They find the body of the victim. His skeleton bears human teeth marks. A lab worker unofficially confirms they match Tooms' dental cast.

Mulder trails Tooms. In one delightfully vile scene, Tooms tosses road kill into his city truck, and then licks his fingers! Muller and Scully stop further attacks, but Tooms uses his amazing stretching abilities, and a pair of stolen shoes, to frame Mulder for brutally beating him.

The pressures of delayed hibernation cause Tooms to lose control and kill the psychiatrist who argued for his release. Muller and Scully track Tooms to his old home. The building has been replaced by a mall.

Tooms still finds a spot to hibernate. He almost kills Mulder but Scully rescues him. Tooms is crushed when his elongated body is caught in the works of an escalator.

A disturbed young girl with psychokinetic powers is the reincarnation of a brutally murdered cop in "Born Again." A tangled web leads Mulder to the solution, aided and hindered by the girl's mother and her psychiatrist.

In "Roland," an aerodynamics researcher is sucked into a Mach 15 wind tunnel. When more scientists die in bizarre ways— one's head is doused in liquid nitrogen and shattered on the floor! — Mulder investigates.

The retarded janitor, Roland, may be committing the crimes while continuing the work of a dead scientist. Mulder discovers that Roland is the brother of the dead scientist. He refuses to believe that the cryogenically frozen head of the dead brother controls Roland!

TRUST NO ONE

The first season finale, "The Erlenmeyer Flask," is a chilling roller coaster ride as government agencies chase an escaped man. The man is the result of human/alien DNA experiments. Mulder is in over his head; Scully makes the DNA connection.

When a warehouse filled with humans in vats is picked clean, Deep Throat reveals himself. He assures Mulder he's about to uncover the truth, but when Mulder tries to rescue the escapee, Mulder's taken captive by a top-secret government group.

Deep Throat gets Scully into a high security research center that stores genetic samples from a 1948 UFO crash. A cryonics container contains a frozen alien, an embryo-like corpse with an over-

sized head and flippered hands.

Scully steals the corpse at Deep Throat's insistence. Mulder is to be traded for the artifact at a nighttime rendezvous.

When Deep Throat hands over the box, the sinister Men In Black shoot him and dump an unconscious Mulder out of their van. Scully is left to ponder Deep Throat's dying words, "Trust no one."

Later, a recovering Mulder and Scully talk on the phone. The X-files department is being shut down; both agents are to be reassigned. The episode ends as the man seen at the close of the first episode enters the same Pentagon warehouse and places the alien in another box among the shelves and shelves of mysterious items.

This is a remarkable way to end a first season! It feels like the end of a series.

Chris Carter and his creative team must find a way to keep Mulder and Scully on the trail of the unknown. It's a safe bet they will. THE X-FILES takes extra steps to establish proper paranoia. What happens on screen always seems much too similar to revelations in the daily news.

THE X-FILES portrays agents at war with a shadow government that writes its own rules and executes them with cruel efficiency. The season finale ends on a foreboding note. The agency is abolished and Deep Throat is dead. Mulder and Scully are on their own now.

They come from out of the past and have been a part of human history for thousands of years. . . .

They are the immortals, and they are among us, some content to live quietly apart while others search out destruction as a normal part of existence. . . .

HIGHLANDER

Immortality has been pondered for ages. Scores of novels dwell on it. Television has offered little of the subject, perhaps only the 1970s short-lived TV series, THE IMMORTAL. Movies have delivered even less.

Then HIGHLANDER came along. The TV series is loosely based on the feature film written by Gregory Widen released in 1985.

HIGHLANDER tells the story of Connor of the clan MacLeod. Hundreds of years ago, the warrior discovered he was immortal. He did not die when he should have after being struck down in battle.

His superstitious brethren drive him from his village. Connor must find his own way in the world after all his friends abandon him.

He doesn't understand his fate until he meets a Spaniard named Ramirez, played by Sean Connery. The Spaniard teaches him the truth about himself and what it means to be immortal. He is also taught there is at least one way he can be killed, by decapitation.

Adrian Paul and Christopher Lambert as seen in the HIGHLANDER pilot, "The Gathering."

Russell Mulcahy directed the film starring Christopher Lambert. It did moderate business in the United States but was a hit in the rest of the world.

The film moves back and forth between the past and the present, telling parallel stories. It employs brilliantly conceived dissolves.

HIGHLANDER II: THE QUICKENING soon followed. It ostensibly picked up where the first film ended. Audiences were dismayed to discover it bore little relation.

The background of the character is altered. Instead of a warrior of the Scottish highlands, Connor becomes an alien revolutionary exiled on Earth 500 years ago. The filmmakers seemed to have thrown out everything that had come before.

In this sequel, Connor supposedly gains immortality as a side-effect of living on Earth, yet the warlord who exiled him is also still alive. He comes to Earth to make life miserable for Connor. It just doesn't make a lick of sense. The filmmakers virtually destroyed the franchise.

Then came the television series. It premiered in the fall of 1992, slightly ahead of the rest of the new pack of science fiction shows. The TV series follows the life of Duncan MacLeod, but Connor makes a guest appearance as a major character in the pilot.

THE HIGHLANDER THROUGH HISTORY

The producers of the feature films, Bill Panzer and Peter Davis, serve as executive producers of the television series. The other executive producers are Marla Ginsburg and Christian Charret of Gaumont Television, France.

The TV show resulted from a business meeting in 1991 between Bill Panzer and Steve Maier, an international television packager. They believed there was a built-in audience for a HIGHLANDER televi-

sion series. The features had been worldwide successes. The films had not been very successful in US theaters, but they were big sellers on home video.

The HIGHLANDER TV series ignored HIGHLANDER II and followed the original film. The television show advances storylines as characters come and go, similar to the approach taken in WISEGUY. It isn't unusual for established characters to suddenly die.

HIGHLANDER is set in our world; its history is our history. The Highlander walked through the centuries, befriending people and saving lives. Duncan MacLeod is not one of the immortals who look down on short-lived mortals. He judges people on their intrinsic worth, not whether an accident of birth made them superhuman.

ENTER ADRIAN PAUL

Adrian Paul plays Duncan MacLeod. The actor was born and raised in London.

SIDEBAR

FIGHTING TECHNIQUES

Swords are an important element in the series. Bob Anderson is the swordmaster. He teaches safety techniques to make it appear performers are striking with full force when the blow actually stops before it hits.

Paul explains, "I did some sword-fighting in WAR OF THE WORLDS, but there's much more involved in this show. It's much more detailed. There are more dives, flips, rolls and so on. It's very intense. The martial arts type of training the Highlanders had is also incorporated, whether it's with a staff or with open hands, aikido, taekwon-do, whatever. I do all my own stuff, except for certain things like gymnastics."

He continues, "It takes a lot of rehearsal because the fighting must be quick and fast. You have to have control of the sword. Many people just swing it, which can be very dangerous. One wrong parry when somebody's following through with a blow, and you can get seriously hurt. I've already been hit on the head and the hands, but that's part of what it is: you can get hurt."

His injuries include five stitches in one finger. He got four stitches on his head when a gun was accidentally dropped onto him during a scene.

He studied Shakespeare and performed in school plays, but his real passion was sports. He played semi-pro soccer, then traveled around Europe as a model. He worked as a dancer and choreographer for six years before moving to Los Angeles and becoming a professional actor.

Paul's first TV role was for THE COLBYS. He portrayed a Russian ballet dancer based on the role Baryshnikov played in the movie WHITE NIGHTS.

After a year on THE COLBYS, he costarred with Tom Berenger in the movie LAST RITES. Paul became the costar, John Kincaid, in the second season of THE WAR OF THE WORLDS when massive cast changes were instituted to save the series. He also made appearances on MURDER, SHE WROTE, BEAUTY AND THE BEAST and in the DARK SHADOWS mini-series.

Adrian Paul was the first actor tested for the role of Duncan MacLeod on HIGHLANDER. The producers couldn't imagine choosing the first actor tested and continued their search. They finally returned to Paul.

The producer explained, "We wanted somebody who could carry the same emotional strengths and liabilities that come with being immortal. We needed somebody to present a sense of world-weariness, yet come across as somebody who hasn't lost his sense of humor."

THE GATHERING

The first episode, "The Gathering," introduced Duncan MacLeod. Christopher Lambert guest starred as Connor MacLeod, tying the film to the television series.

At first no one knew whether Christopher Lambert would be available for "The Gathering." The script was revised several times, delaying production. Everyone wanted to enhance continuity by including Christopher Lambert as Connor MacLeod.

Before it was clear if Lambert would appear, one script draft cast Adrian

Paul as Connor MacLeod. If that had appeared, Connor would have continued as the protagonist of the series.

Christopher Lambert added to the marketability of the new series when it premiered. He is much more prominent than Adrian Paul.

The series has now developed its own fan following. Paul has become just as popular as Christopher Lambert among HIGHLANDER fans.

ON LOCATION IN CANADA AND FRANCE

A HIGHLANDER season runs 22 episodes. The series is filmed in Vancouver, British Columbia, Canada and Paris, France. Like most of the science fiction on television today, it is distributed through first-run syndication.

The series does not air on a network such as ABC or Fox, but is sold to local stations. It appears on different days in different cities. Some cities air the series in prime time. Others, including Los Angeles, air it late at night due to the violence of the series.

The HIGHLANDER television series began in the Fall of 1992 with a rousing story introducing Adrian Paul as Duncan MacLeod. Duncan MacLeod is not a loner like the Highlander of the original films. He has both mortal and immortal friends. Occasionally they are involved in intrigues involving Duncan's ancient enemies.

Paul says, "Duncan likes to evoke feelings from other people. He deals with the world and has fun with what he does, but he's a deep character who has many problems and is lonely. He doesn't wear it on his sleeve."

Paul continued, "He enjoys the life he leads, because otherwise there would be no point. He wouldn't be an immortal. He would just give up the fight and get another immortal to kill him."

AN EVOLVING CHARACTER

The first motion picture gave the Highlander a

TOP: Ritchie Ryan (Stan Kirsh) of HIGHLANDER.
BOTTOM: Phillip Akin as Charlie DeSalvo and Jim Byrnes as Joe Dawson, semi-regulars on HIGH-LANDER.

Photo ©1994 Rysher.TPE

past, and a sense of mysticism. He is part of the human race and its history. This mysticism is lost if he's an alien from another planet.

The actor feels that Duncan MacLeod changed as the series progressed and he brought elements of his own personality to the portrayal. He says, "I think it happens a lot with characters in a series. The writer's character will be one way in the beginning and then when the actor comes in and starts playing it, the character changes because the actor brings something to the character that is uniquely his. That is why Duncan is much more human on the show this year."

Adrian Paul told the producers he wanted informal dialogue so Duncan could have quick exchanges with other characters. "Actors bring something to a role, which is why people watch," he explained. "If an actor doesn't bring something of their own and make that role his, then no one is going to be interested in it."

He adds, "Whenever Duncan is around, his morals are very similar to mine. Whenever you do a role, a part of you has to be in that role, otherwise you can't justify it."

WHO ARE THE WATCHERS?

Jim Byrnes plays Joe Dawson, the head of The Watchers. The secret group of mortals keeps tabs on the immortals.

Duncan doesn't know if he can trust Dawson. The Watchers consider the immortals a threat to humankind, but honor a truce of sorts. Dawson has seen Duncan MacLeod fight against evil immortals who threaten humanity.

The Watchers were introduced in the second season. They will continue in the third season.

Byrnes grew up in St. Louis. He led a varied childhood. He still enjoys playing the blues guitar, a hobby he began when he was 13. At 15 he performed Shakespeare in the Park. Byrnes studied for the priesthood, and later attended Boston University and St. Louis University.

He lost both legs in a car accident in 1972. It didn't interfere with his desire to be an actor.

His first regular role was on the hit series WISEGUY. His disability was incorporated into his character. Byrnes other work includes THE HAT SQUAD, HARMONY CATS, DIRTY WORKS, LIGHTNING FORCE, NEON RIDER, THE OMEN 4, IN THE BEST INTEREST OF THE CHILD, DANGER BAY and THE HITCHHIKER.

The character Byrnes plays in HIGHLANDER will be expanded for the third season. He appeared in the most crucial story arcs of the second season, including "Unholy Alliance" and "The Counterfeit." His talent as a blues musician will be highlighted during the third season.

NEW FRIENDS

A new character was introduced in the second

season of HIGHLANDER. Charlie DeSalvo is played by Philip Akin.

DeSalvo owns a martial arts studio below the loft where Duncan MacLeod lives. The actor actually holds a fourth degree black belt in Yoshinkan Aikido. He also studies Tai Chi and Kung Fu near his Toronto home.

Akin brings a variety of film credits, including PANIC IN THE CITY, STELLA, DEVLIN, FX2, and DESCENDING ANGELS. TV credits include work as a regular for the first season of the WAR OF THE WORLDS, TOP COPS, NIGHT HEAT, JUDGE, and BIZARRE, a Canadian series.

Originally the producers wanted Duncan to reveal his true nature to Charlie. Adrian Paul opposed this, telling TV GUIDE, "Here's a man who could barely tell the woman he loved what he was—he certainly wouldn't announce it to a new friend."

Ritchie Ryan, revealed to be an immortal in the second season of HIGHLANDER, is played by Stan Kirsch. Stan moved to Los Angeles to pursue acting after appearing in commercials when he was much younger. He attended Duke University as a political science major while studying acting. He says, "I went through the whole spectrum of acting, movement and voice work, which was all geared toward Shakespeare and regional theater."

He worked in regional theater in summer stock. "I made $24 a night to perform in a play six times a week in the mountains of North Carolina," he recalled. "It was the greatest summer I'd ever had and I couldn't get rid of the acting bug."

After graduating from Duke University, he pursued acting as a profession. His credits include appearances on GENERAL HOSPITAL and TRUE COLORS as well as starring in THE STREETS OF BEVERLY HILLS, a pilot for ABC.

A YOUNG IMMORTAL

Adrian Paul says his character knew Ritchie was an immortal all along. He would have known it from the recognition feeling immortals have when they meet.

Ritchie's immortality factor wasn't fully active at the time. He would have experienced the feeling without knowing what it meant. He didn't know anything about the immortals until Duncan told him.

Ritchie changes in dramatic ways during the storyline involving Tessa's death. Adrian Paul explains, "You see Ritchie's character was very useful for Duncan. He was a friend. There are two ways of looking at it. If you didn't make him immortal, why was he hanging around Duncan, and if he is immortal how can he hang around Duncan? At least now Duncan can teach him. He is trying to teach him how to be immortal. Duncan's now become what Christopher Lambert or Connor MacLeod was to Duncan MacLeod."

Ritchie is naive but learning on the job. Ritchie proves himself in "The Counterfeit." When Horton tries to assassinate Dawson, Ritchie intercepts three bullets meant for him.

He "dies" again and then revives. It should be noted that although immortals cannot die from conventional means and recover quickly from major wounds, they still feel pain. They just bounce back in a way no mortal could.

THE HISTORY OF DUNCAN MACLEOD

Duncan cut himself off from other immortals for 120 years, until Connor MacLeod told him the Gathering was taking place. He lived with a tribe of American Indians. A warring tribe murdered his wife.

In modern times Duncan is happily living with Tessa Noel, his lover for 15 years. Duncan MacLeod was born 400 years ago in the Highlands of Scotland. He became immortal in 1622.

When the show premiered in 1992, Duncan was nearing his 400th birthday. Tessa referred to

Alexandra Vandernoot as Tessa Noel and Adrian Paul as Duncan MacLeod in the TV series HIGH-LANDER.

Photo ©1994 Rysher.TPE

this in the first episode. Over the centuries Duncan has been a newspaperman, a gentleman, and a warrior.

"The Gathering" reveals how Connor taught Duncan MacLeod to live as an immortal. Like Connor, Duncan was banished from his tribe when he arose from the dead after being killed in battle. Connor's friends now know him as Mac while other immortals call him "The Highlander." His relationship with his father is revealed in "Family Tree."

THE STRUGGLE AMONG IMMORTALS

The focus of the TV series is on the struggle between good immortals and evil immortals. The movie concept that in the end there can be only one immortal left alive remains, but it isn't an ongoing concern.

All immortals who meet eventually fight a duel to the death in the original HIGHLANDER movie. That is not true in the TV series.

Immortals can only be killed by beheading. When one immortal slays another, they receive the other's power in a mystical process called "The Quickening." According to HIGHLANDER II, immortals came from outer space. This is ignored by the TV series. Production notes answer this question in the following way:

"The origin of Immortals has not been explained and very likely never will be. Beings from outer space? What beings from outer space?"

Clearly Davis-Panzer Productions, makers of both HIGHLANDER films and the TV series, have had second thoughts. Producer Bill Panzer defended HIGHLANDER II: THE QUICKENING in the December 1992 issue of STARLOG. He said, "I always felt HIGHLANDER 2 was a success in terms of telling an exciting, entertaining story and furthering the HIGHLANDER odyssey. To this point, the HIGHLANDER films in the US are more of a cult

thing, and the second film drew upon that cult. But I'm convinced that these films will eventually break through to the kind of audience in the United States that they have elsewhere in the world."

THE FATE OF TESSA NOEL

The TV series introduced new things to the mythos. The Watchers are new to the TV series. Holy Ground of any religion is a sanctuary. They will not fight in sacred locations.

Immortals cannot gang up on each other—fights must be individual. Immortals sense when another immortal is nearby. Immortals cannot have children, although this is biological not a pact.

Immortals live among humanity undetected. Occasionally journalists happen on the truth, so Duncan MacLeod must avoid them.

During the first season, Duncan lived with his mortal lover, Tessa Noel, played by Alexandra Vandernoot. She is a

Frenchwoman. They resided above his antique store where Tessa worked as a sculptress and curator.

Early in the second season, Tessa and Ritchie escape from one of Duncan's enemies only to be shot down in the street by a thug in a random act of violence. Tessa died but Ritchie returned to life.

No one knows if they are immortal until they are "killed" and do not die. An immortal ages normally until they "die." Only then does the immortality factor emerge and aging stop. This is why some immortals look older than others. Duncan was in his thirties when his immortality emerged.

TURNING POINT

Tessa Noel's death was very controversial among fans. Duncan and Tessa made a perfect couple who truly loved each other. Occasionally Duncan thinks of Tessa in a flashback.

The actress who played Tessa chose to leave the show to spend more time with her family in Europe. The death of her character became necessary. Shortly after she left the series a decision was made to film several episodes in France allowing her to make a return appearance in "The Counterfeit."

After Tessa's death, Duncan sells his antique store and moves into an industrial loft over a Dojo. Serious martial artists and warriors train in the loft.

Duncan returns to France in the second season. He moves into a houseboat and stories center in Paris for awhile. Duncan leaves the city at the end of the second season to return to the United States.

Duncan MacLeod set himself up as a protector of mortals from the ravages of immortals. Some immortals look down on mortals because their lives are so brief. To an immortal, a normal life span seems to be that of a housefly.

Not all immortals believe this. Some immortals marry mortals they love knowing they will watch them die.

Adrian Paul enjoys seeing these issues in a story. He describes it as "the moral and ethical implications that face an immortal character—how you handle relationships with people you know you're going to outlive."

Some episodes illustrate the approach of the series. Although the motion pictures emphasize action and plot over character, the TV series develops characters with personalities.

OLD FRIENDS

In "The Fighter," Duncan MacLeod meets an immortal friend. Tommy Sullivan is played by Bruce Weitz, a former regular on HILL STREET BLUES. He is the manager of a boxer.

The story first appears to be a typical tale of crooked boxing when Sully's fighter is wooed by a wealthy promoter. Duncan invests in the boxer's future to protect him from the seedy promoter and his gang.

Sully is not your average immortal. He is shy and a bit innocent. He can't talk to women and doesn't have much money. Unlike Duncan MacLeod, Sully hasn't learned to save money over the centuries.

Duncan is deeply troubled when the crooked boxing promoter turns up dead. When George, Sully's boxer and old friend, decides to go with someone else, Sully kills him as well.

Duncan asks Sully if he kills everyone who cheats him. Sully casually admits that he does. "We kill people all the time— it's what we do," he calmly says.

It is suddenly clear that the likable lug is homicidal. He has no respect for life.

Most episodes build up to a confrontation in which Duncan's opponent loses his head. This time it's Sully.

Duncan finds fighting a friend difficult. At the climax, it's unclear whether he'll make the final deadly strike. When he does, he doesn't act as if he's won a battle but lost a friend.

THE MUMMY

Duncan MacLeod encounters two thugs trying to rob a truck in "Pharaoh's Daughter."

SIDEBAR

SIDEBAR

THE MERCHANDISE

The original HIGH-LANDER motion picture offered excellent original music composed by the rock group Queen. Although Queen faded from the rock scene by the late '80s, their music made a comeback in 1992. This coincided with the premiere of the HIGHLANDER television series. It uses their song, "Princes of the Universe," as the series theme.

There is no HIGH-LANDER soundtrack album. Instead Queen's A KIND OF MAGIC includes "Princes of the Universe" and "Who Wants To Live Forever" along with other music associated with the HIGH-LANDER movie and television series.

Two videotapes

When the truck passes him, he feels the familiar sensation of a nearby immortal.

Foiling the thieves, he approaches a huge crate that opens to reveal an Egyptian sarcophagus. Inside the sarcophagus is a mummy. Inside the wrapping is a living woman.

Nefertiri is the former handmaiden of Cleopatra. Knowing she was an immortal, when Cleopatra committed suicide Nefertiri took a sleeping potion. She was buried in the same tomb as her beloved queen.

Two thousand years later Duncan MacLeod unwraps her. Nefertiri emerges nude.

Nefertiri should only speak Egyptian, not English. This is never dealt with as she speaks perfect English from the moment she awakens. It is never hinted that MacLeod teaches her English.

Nefertiri doesn't know she's slept for two thousand years. MacLeod teaches her about her new world.

OLD ADVERSARIES

She meets Marcus Constantine in a museum. He is an immortal Roman soldier she knew in Egypt. They were lovers two millennia ago.

She blames him for betraying her queen, causing Cleopatra's suicide. Her queen was Nefertiri's world and she wants vengeance.

MacLeod arranges a peace conference between Constantine and Nefertiri. Marcus explains he was a Roman soldier two thousand years before, but he's an historian now. "I used to make history," he says. "Now I try to make sure it survives."

He's a changed man. He hopes Nefertiri will recognize that both his Rome and her queen are long gone.

While MacLeod visits Constantine, a man slips aboard MacLeod's boat and confronts Nefertiri. He's a Watcher sworn to kill immortals to protect humanity.

He vows to kill Nefertiri, then MacLeod and Constantine. He calls

Nefertiri an abomination. She slays the man.

Duncan and Nefertiri have a peaceful dinner at Constantine's home. She goes into the kitchen to talk to Angela, Marcus' wife.

Nefertiri recognizes that Constantine loves her and murders Angela to punish Marcus. In the shocking scene, Nefertiri casually stabs Angela to death, then announces the deed to Marcus, who is overcome with grief.

Immortals feel normal emotions and can be injured or knocked unconscious. They just cannot be killed unless decapitated.

CLASH OF SWORDS

Nefertiri and Duncan had become lovers. After the murder, he throws her out. She cannot understand his actions.

She accuses him of betraying her since she had every right to exact vengeance against Constantine. Duncan insists her fight was with Marcus, not Angela. He will not tolerate immor-tals using mortals as pawns in their conflicts.

After Angela's funeral, Nefertiri appears at the cemetery. She confronts Marcus and Duncan.

Marcus won't fight her even if it costs his own life. Duncan won't allow it. He engages Nefertiri in combat.

Duncan and Nefertiri duel to the death. He questions whether she can kill a lover, but she proves willing. Duncan defends himself and slays the handmaiden of Cleopatra.

Audiences suspected this character would replace Tessa in Duncan's life. The first half of the episode seemed to confirm this. That is why Nefertiri's betrayal of Duncan's trust when she slays Angela is such a surprise.

Immortals carry swords in these episodes. The swords don't appear until a challenge is issued when, suddenly, the immortals draw their swords from. . . somewhere. And these aren't short swords, either.

from the television series have been released. HIGH-LANDER: THE GATHERING con-tains the pilot episode plus the first season's "Revenge Is Sweet." There is also addition-al footage not in the aired versions.

The two-part episode, "Unholy Alliance," from the second season was slated to be released in the spring of '94. There are plans to release additional episodes on video.

No HIGH-LANDER novels have appeared in the United States. A nov-elization written by Gary Douglas from the original motion picture was published by Severn House Publishers, Ltd. in England (ISBN #0-7278-1396-X).

Plans are underway for novelizations based on TV episodes. Nothing is final yet.

There's even a Highlander Fan Club. They can be contacted by writing to: The Gathering, P.O. Box 123, Aurora, CO. 80040.

Then there are the swords. Marto USA provides some swords to the Highlander series. They sell replicas of MacLeod's sword along with others used in the series.

A North Carolina company, Swordmasters, is a licensed American dealer for Marto. It offers the Katana sword for approximately $250. Swordmasters can be contacted at P.O. Box 124, Garner, North Carolina 27529. These are genuine hard metal swords, not aluminum or wooden replicas.

HISTORICAL CONNECTIONS

The stories involve Duncan with immortals he knew in previous centuries. Duncan meets Nicholas Ward again in "The Vampire."

Centuries ago, Ward created the legend of the vampire by draining blood from human bodies and leaving marks on their necks. He likes to kill.

Ward is up to his serial killer tricks in modern Paris. Duncan is determined to end the curse of the vampire.

Duncan meets a modern day dictator in "Warmonger." The immortal subjected human beings to torture throughout history.

Drakov worked for the Czar in 19th Century Russia. Duncan persuaded Drakov to free prisoners in exchange for a vow never to kill him. Since immortals fear only other immortals, Drakov considered this important.

In an interesting scene, Drakov robs a family of their home and property. Duncan steals a pouch of jewels from Drakov to help his friends start again in another land although he knows he'll never see them again.

A century later, Duncan meets Drakov in Canada. Drakov barely escapes an assassination attempt. He had run a concentration camp in World War Two. The elderly assassin's family was executed in the camp.

Duncan tells Drakov to leave the dying man alone. Instead Drakov has his thugs kill the man. Duncan dishonors his vow and kills Drakov. Characterization plays a large part in this effective story.

A LEGEND TO DIE FOR

In the "Legacy," an immortal named Luther slays an immortal named Rebecca. She had been his teacher.

He kills her because he wants a crystal she is wearing. There are three such crystals. Luther believes that when they are joined, they will grant invincibility.

Amanda, an immortal Duncan previously encountered, was a friend of Rebecca. She tells him what happened. Duncan tracks down Luther and kills him.

Luther had secured two of the crystals. He refuses to reveal their location, but Duncan says he doesn't care.

The episode never reveals if the crystal is genuine. Duncan doesn't believe it is.

Rebecca never told Amanda the significance of the crystals although they were close friends for centuries. A flashback reveals that Rebecca helped Amanda discover her true nature and learn how to prepare for life as an immortal. They even met Duncan a couple hundred years before.

THE RETURN OF RITCHIE RYAN

Ritchie Ryan returns in "Prodigal Son." He's being chased by an immortal searching for Duncan MacLeod.

This immortal, Martin Hyde, is different. He kills only "seasoned" immortals, not young ones.

Duncan first met Hyde 250 years before. Then, the man had no interest in Duncan MacLeod. He wanted to find Connor MacLeod.

Ritchie hadn't appeared since shortly after Tessa was killed. Ritchie and Mac had parted under difficult circumstances. They've since made up.

Mac helps Ritchie when Hyde frames him for murder. In one scene Mac sets up Hyde to be captured by the police by agreeing to meet him and not bringing his sword. The police see a madman waving a sword trying to kill Duncan. Hyde is shot and falls from the roof of a building.

He revives in the morgue, retrieves his sword, and goes after Duncan. Mac is nervous about the confrontation, but wins anyway.

Adrian Paul as Duncan MacLeod, The Highlander.

Photo ©1994 Rysher.TPE

THE RETURN OF TESSA NOEL?

The season finale of HIGHLANDER was a special two-part episode, "Counterfeit." The storyline featured the return of Horton, the mortal stalking Duncan.

Horton escaped after being shot in the conclusion of "Unholy Alliance." In "Counterfeit," he engineers deadly mind games to exploit people who know what he wants, but not how far he'll go to get it.

Horton sets up a young man named Pete to seemingly rescue Ritchie from The Watchers. Mac is suspicious. Comparative novice Ritchie is annoyed Mac doesn't trust Pete.

Meanwhile Horton kidnaps a woman being transferred between prisons. He persuades her to have her features surgically altered.

Meilani Paul, the wife of Adrian Paul, plays the woman. They have no scenes together. By the time Duncan meets this woman, she looks like someone else— someone very familiar to HIGH-LANDER fans.

Part one of this story has two climaxes. When Pete is shot to death, it supposedly proves he was on the level. This drives a wedge between Ritchie and Duncan.

Pete worked for Horton, but had no idea how his boss intended to use him to further his plans. "Divide and conquer," as Horton puts it.

Then, when the bandages come off the young woman, she is suddenly a double for Tessa Noel! Alexandra Vandernoot even plays the role of the altered woman.

FACING THE FUTURE

In part two, Duncan has a couple of "chance" meetings with this woman. She claims her name is Lisa.

They develop a relationship because Duncan can't bring himself to walk away from this woman who looks just like Tessa. When Ritchie meets the woman, he's surprised. In a twist on part one, Ritchie

warns Duncan it is all too convenient and Duncan won't listen.

Later Duncan wonders if he's accepting her because he doesn't want to doubt his good fortune. That's when Lisa is "kidnapped" and Horton plays more head games with Duncan.

During a confrontation in the cemetery, Duncan persuades Lisa to help him. Horton murders her before Duncan's eyes.

The episode doesn't end on a cliffhanger. Duncan kills Horton. No immortals are slain in either episode, so there's no beheading of the week.

"Counterfeit" depends on character interaction. There are even flashbacks to the real Tessa, including when Duncan revealed to her that he's an immortal.

There's a steamy love scene between Mac and Lisa with many close-ups and montages. Fans who hated to see Tessa go get her back again, if only briefly.

The episode ends when Mac sells his barge in Paris to move on to another country. Ritchie goes with him.

The third season of HIGHLANDER is now in production. Viewers will learn where they headed in September 1994.

As HIGHLANDER awaits its third season as a television series, the third film, HIGHLANDER III: THE MAGICIAN, appeared in the summer of 1994. Christopher Lambert returned to play Connor MacLeod for the third time on the big screen.

HIGHLANDER lives on in both TV and theatrical incarnations, just like an immortal warrior should.

May of 1994 saw the end of seven successful years of STAR TREK—THE NEXT GENERATION, but the future isn't over yet.

by W.D. Kilpack III

NEXT GENERATION WARPS FROM TV TO THE SILVER SCREEN

After seven years, the number one syndicated hour-long drama, STAR TREK—THE NEXT GENERATION, is moving from TV to the big screen. After 178 episodes accumulated 16 Emmy Awards from 46 nominations, and a Peabody Award, the two-hour grand finale appeared the week of May 23, 1994. Paramount, the studio behind STAR TREK, hopes to bring 20 million regular TV viewers into the theaters to see the crew of the Enterprise in the larger-than-life magic of movies.

The crew of NCC-1701-D culminates twenty-eight years of STAR TREK ideals in the original series, films, and a staggering number of novels. Gene Roddenberry, creator and executive producer of STAR TREK and STAR TREK—THE NEXT GENERATION, always believed mankind will evolve beyond the limitations of base desires.

The major players of STAR TREK: THE NEXT GENERA-TION.

Photo c 1994

Paramount Pictures

Roddenberry once said, "The collective commitment of our nations, as well as the vision, wisdom, and hard work of many, many individuals will be required to bring our dreams into fruition. In a way, the Enterprise and the optimistic future in which it exists, might be thought of as a reminder of what we can achieve when we really try."

NEXT GENERATION's Capt. Jean-Luc Picard, played by Patrick Stewart, epitomizes the ideal. He holds duty above all else. Picard discards desires of the flesh when they conflict with duty to ship, crew, and Starfleet.

Although he works alongside Dr. Beverly Crusher, played by Gates McFadden, and obviously finds her very attractive, he never shows his feelings. Instead he takes a paternal role towards her son, child prodigy Wesley, played by Wil Wheaton. Picard helps him develop into a strong individual and Academy cadet.

Picard is a good, just man. He is also a consummate professional.

KIRK AND PICARD

William Shatner plays James Tiberius Kirk very differently. The captain of the Enterprise in the original STAR TREK embodies the adventurous spirit of man reaching out into the depths of space for the first time. He is the kind of adventurer that explored the American West.

Instinct and gut impulse ride herd. Caution is often thrown to the wind. Kirk lives his passions with indomitable will.

A man like Picard had to follow in the footsteps of trailblazer Kirk. Kirk carves his way into unknown space taming new frontiers. The logical Picard settles where Kirk leads, establishing peace and the rule of law.

The two-hour finale of NEXT GENERATION revealed much about Picard, and hailed back to the series pilot, "Encounter at Farpoint." The finale also offered the reappearance of Q.

With the finale, the NEXT GENERATION TV series achieved a sense of completion, circling back to its pilot while moving the story forward with enticing possibilities for the future.

THE MEASURE OF A MAN

The NEXT GENERATION lacks the whirlwind action of the original series. It adds new elements of equal interest instead.

Data triggers the exploration for the definition of life. Artificial intelligence is a keystone in man's quest for knowledge. A truly intelligent being created by man raises many questions. Philosophers, theologians, and scientists all bring arguments to the debate.

If the soul is the seat of intelligence created by God how can it be replicated with wires and microchips? If intelligence can be artificially created why do souls exist?

Data crystalizes this debate. The android learns

and makes decisions. He serves as second officer aboard the flagship of Starfleet.

The debate is the central plot of episodes, including "The Measure of a Man." A Starfleet trial determines if Data is a sentient being or Starfleet property. Despite the ruling in his favor, Data lacks emotions.

His brother, Lore, also played by Brent Spiner, is a replica of Data, but with emotions. Lore's man-made emotions seem unable to function in moderation. He is either in a killing fury or drunkenly happy.

In "Brothers," Dr. Noonian Soong, the creator of both androids, tells Data that Lore is flawed. The character is yet another portrayal by Brent Spiner.

Soong says Data is perfect, possessing a mind more capable than that of a Vulcan. Data also shows physical capabilities beyond those of humankind. Yet he is constantly curious.

Data experiments with the crew, trying to appear human. His innocent curiosity is endearing. The successful Starfleet officer asks questions expected of a four-year-old.

Data changes during the series. In the final episode, "All Good Things. . . ," it is clear that the Data of "Encounter At Farpoint" is much stiffer than he is seven years later.

DATA'S EQUAL

In the excellent "Elementary, Dear Data," Geordi La Forge, played by LaVar Burton, programs the holodeck to create a being capable of defeating Data. The computer generates a new Dr. Moriarty in a Sherlock Holmes-style world. Moriarty is an artificial super intelligence with a holographic body.

Moriarty kidnaps Dr. Katherine Pulaski, played by Diana Muldaur, to force the Enterprise crew to grant him life outside the holodeck. He uses the holodeck to gain limited control of the Enterprise.

Picard accedes to his demands. Moriarty relinquishes control when Picard promises to preserve the holodeck program in which he was created. One day, when man knows how to make holograms real, he will have a physical body.

Moriarty releases Pulaski and allows the holodeck to be turned off. This powerful philosophical and emotional play is a keynote in NEXT GENERATION's success.

"In Theory" is another excellent episode. Data takes a human lover, Jenna D'Sora, played by Michele Scarabelli, a security officer aboard the Enterprise. D'Sora had recently emerged from a bad relationship with a brutal, unfeeling man. She is on the rebound.

Data becomes affectionate as she works alongside him on the ship. He sees an opportunity to explore human emotions and asks Counselor Deanna Troi, played by Marina Sirtis, if he should pursue courtship rituals with the

At the helm of the Enterprise on STAR TREK: THE NEXT GENERATION.

Captain Picard discusses a plan with Data on STAR TREK: THE NEXT GENERATION.

Photo c 1994 Paramount Pictures

woman. Troi thinks it would be good for him.

COUNTERPOINTS

Commander William Riker, played by Jonathan Frakes, suggests giving flowers. Data fills the woman's quarters with exotic flowers, sings to her, and meets her nightly for dinner.

She finally decides it's all a mistake; that she traded an unfeeling man for one physically incapable of feeling. She anguishes over telling him. When she does, he replies, "Oh. In that case, I will erase the program."

He looks down and picks up his cat, as if nothing has happened. It is a very moving — although disturbing — scene.

Lieutenant Worf balances Data's lack of passion. The Klingon serves as security chief and third officer aboard the Enterprise. He is the first Klingon to hold such high Starfleet position.

Roddenberry described Worf as "a symbol of the reduction of global tensions in the world today." His conception of duty is as rigid as that of Data and Picard.

Worf has trouble controlling his naturally volatile disposition. Klingons are a warrior race. Worf, although raised by humans, wants to be a true Klingon and a good Starfleet officer.

Worf hides his feelings. He is very alone in the Federation, trusting his own instincts to find answers to his problems.

Data's android charm grows from Spock's logical predisposition. Worf is uncharted territory. He offers a dark side to Roddenberry's bright vision of mankind's evolution.

WORF DECIDES

"Parallels" shows Worf in crisis. Returning from a "batleff" tournament, he passes through a quantum rift where barriers between realities are weak. When LaForge's VISOR emits an energy pulse, Worf blinks from one possible future to another.

The most startling possible future is not when the Borg destroy the Federation, but when Worf is first officer aboard the Enterprise. In this possibility, Riker is captain, Picard is dead, and Deanna Troi is Worf's loving, affectionate wife.

This possible reality helps Worf recognize his attraction to her. It shakes his conception of himself. He is tempted not to return to his true space-time continuum but instead continue his life with Troi and their two children.

This shows a neglected side of Worf. Even when his son, Alexander, is present, there is no strong focus on Worf's tender side. Worf is protective and proud, but troubled with his role as a single father in "New Ground" and "Cost of Living."

He finally rejects remaining in the alternate reality because of Alexander. In that time stream, Alexander does not exist. The need to return to stabilize the quantum fissure removes the decision from his shoulders.

Upon leaving, he takes Troi in his arms for a passionate kiss. Returning to his own Enterprise, he asks Troi to have dinner with him, beginning with champagne. This would have been an interesting development to follow.

EQUAL TIME

Different NEXT GENERATION characters are emphasized in different episodes. This is a key strength the original STAR TREK lacked. There are no one-dimensional protagonists in NEXT GENERATION.

Riker reeks of military tradition. He also harbors self-doubts, refusing command on three starships, the Drake, Aries, and Melbourne. He operates from gut instinct, as illustrated in "Peak Performance."

Troi is gentle and caring. Her big, puppy-dog eyes add to her patient listening when officers explain their problems. She typifies the perfect psychologist. Her opinion is highly regarded when for diplomacy.

She is also a lieutenant commander. She ably commands the Enterprise in a volatile situation in "Disaster" and becomes an effective subversive aboard a Romulan vessel in "Face of the Enemy."

LaForge is young and excitable. He performs his duties with a maturity beyond the scope of his years. He has the best sense of humor, but displays great strength when forced to work with a Romulan on a hostile planet in "The Enemy."

THE FUTURE OF STAR TREK

NEXT GENERATION builds on the foundation laid by the original series and movies. Rick Berman, current executive producer of the NEXT GENERATION series and movie said, "STAR TREK as a phenomenon, has existed for [twenty-eight] years now. Seventy-nine episodes of the original series; [six] motion pictures; NEXT GENERA-

TION with [178] episodes. During these [twenty-eight] years, the rules and laws of STAR TREK have been forged and scrutinized, perhaps more than those of any other television series in history."

This series is stronger than any other science fiction program. It focuses on the bright future birthed by Roddenberry. As man answers critical questions about the nature of existence he continues to unearth greater mysteries. Mankind never ceases the quest for answers. Roddenberry said, "On STAR TREK, we've tried to show technology not as important in itself, but as a tool with which we humans can better reach for our dreams."

A QUEST ACROSS TIME

STAR TREK: GENERATIONS began filming in late March 1994. It builds from STAR TREK VI, when the original crew passes the reins.

Three characters from the original series appear: Kirk, Montgomery Scott, played by James Doohan, and Pavel Chekov, portrayed by Walter Koenig. They appear for about twenty minutes.

Rumors abound. One insists Kirk will die.

Mr. Scott appeared in NEXT GENERATION in "Relics." He was on a ship that crashed. Scotty kept himself alive by setting the transporter on a loop, maintaining his physical pattern in teleporter-induced suspended animation.

It will be interesting to see more interaction between Geordi and Scotty. In "Relics," Mr. Scott asked Geordi why he reported exactly how quickly something could be done without exaggerating. It gave a chuckle and could be good for a laugh or three in the film.

It is not clear how Kirk and Picard will meet. The NEXT GENERATION takes places seventy-five years after Classic Trek. Berman has given a hint: "The story will bridge two centuries."

The company producing the film issued a statement. According to

Paramount Pictures, the film will depict a "unique astronomical phenomenon" bringing together different times. Picard and Kirk will meet face-to-face in the 24th Century.

GENERATIONS TO COME

More films of the NEXT GENERATION are inevitable. There were six with the original STAR TREK crew.

Future films will probably include such mainstays in the STAR TREK universe as Spock, played by Leonard Nimoy, now an occasional character in the NEXT GENERATION TV series. Spock is shaking the very Federation with his radical work as an ambassador to Romulus.

What of Dr. Leonard McCoy? Or, more properly, Admiral McCoy?

The good doctor, played by DeForest Kelley, appeared in the pilot episode of NEXT GENERATION. He was 147 years old. If he lived to be 147, he could live long enough to be in a NEXT GENERATION film or two.

Sulu, played by George Takei, and Chekov could also appear. Both were key players in the original series who were just coming into their own in the movies.

Takei has expressed a desire to continue in STAR TREK films. As of the sixth film, he was captain of the Excelsior. He should still be alive. The Excelsior must have accomplished some big things to be the model adopted for NCC-1701-B.

Despite the splendid send-off NEXT GENERATION received with its concluding episode, the story of the crew of the Enterprise 1701-D is far from over. It will resume on course for the big screen in November 1994.

STAR TREK—THE NEXT GENERATION is heading for the big screen. DEEP SPACE NINE must maintain the franchise for TV as STAR TREK VOYAGE prepares to burst on the scene.

STAR TREK—DEEP SPACE NINE

The third incarnation of STAR TREK premiered in January 1993. The bold move was announced shortly after the death of STAR TREK creator Gene Roddenberry in 1991. Paramount set the series in the STAR TREK universe without following the template established in 1966. This STAR TREK would offer no huge spaceship or crew of intrepid adventures going "where no man has gone before."

Originally DEEP SPACE NINE was to be "darker and grittier" than other STAR TREK. That proved only relative. Many episodes of STAR TREK—THE NEXT GENERATION are as dark and gritty as the grimmest episode of DEEP SPACE NINE.

What sets DEEP SPACE NINE apart is its fixed locale every week. It only deals with familiar cultures, including Romulans and Ferengi twice a season.

The major players of DEEP SPACE NINE.

Photo c 1994 Paramount Pictures

THE COMMAND CREW

Press materials set DEEP SPACE NINE in the year 2360 AD., contemporary with THE NEXT GENERATION. Deep Space Nine is a space station orbiting Bajor. That region of space is the focal point of every story.

Some episodes follow one or more central character through the wormhole into the Gamma Quadrant, encountering new planets and cultures. Most episodes remain on the space station.

Commander Benjamin Sisko and his son, Jake, are the two most pivotal characters. They are from Earth. Ben's wife and Jake's mother, Jennifer, was killed by the Borg at the battle of Wolf 359.

Ostensibly second in command, Major Kira Nerys is primarily the Bajoran liaison. She was a member of the Bajoran underground involved in anti-Cardassian activities until they withdrew from Bajor. The character was created when Michelle Forbes turned down the chance to play Ensign Ro for the series.

Nerys and Dax are different from STAR TREK— THE NEXT GENERATION characters. They are strong females, a rarity on THE NEXT GENERATION and the original STAR TREK. Kira and Dax lead missions, unlike Deanna Troi and Beverly Crusher.

Odo is the security officer, a position he also occupied under the Cardassians. Odo was not a collaborator, but a neutral able to act as a buffer between the Cardassians and the Bajorans.

THE OPERATIONS CREW

Dr. Julian Bashir is a recent graduate of Starfleet Medical. Deep Space Nine offers him the opportunity to practice medicine in the far frontiers of space. He was naive at first but quickly learned his role.

Jadzia Dax is a Trill, a symbiont who merged with an alien life form into a dual persona. The young woman is the new Dax, following Curzon Dax, an old man. Jadzia possesses the combined memories of all previous versions of Dax, which go back several hundred years.

Miles O'Brien is the Chief of Operations. He was promoted to Deep Space Nine from the Enterprise. He has rebuilt key systems trashed by the Cardassians when they evacuated the station. Miles is only a few years older than Julian Bashir, but sometimes feels competitive with the younger man. His wife, Keiko, doesn't share this view.

Keiko O'Brien married Miles when they were both still stationed on the Enterprise. She gave birth to their daughter, Molly, aboard that starship. Keiko has started a school for children on the space station, although Bajoran children sometimes create problems. Her teachings sometimes conflict with their religion, particularly concerning the wormhole and the Prophets.

The Ferengi, Quark, was aboard Deep Space Nine before the Federation came.

Photo c 1994 Paramount Pictures

MEET THE ALIENS

Quark was aboard Deep Space Nine before the Federation came. The Ferengi businessman is lecherous and dishonest but comes through in a pinch. The seemingly contradictory traits create an unusual character.

Semi-regulars include Quark's brother, Rom, and his son, Nog, Quark's nephew. Nog and Jake are close friends. Jake privately tutors Nog.

The Grand Nagus appeared in two episodes. He opposes Ferengi children being educated by the Federation. Nog disagrees; he recognizes that knowledge is power.

The Vedeks appear infrequently. They are venerated members of the Bajoran religious order. When Kai Opaka was forced to remain on a small world inside the Gamma Quadrant, a new Kai was chosen. This is a long, complicated process. Ultimately Vedek Winn became the new Kai despite her opposition to the Federation.

She has been involved in shady incidents, including an assassination plot against her chief rival. Kai Winn will be a dangerous opponent in future stories. She now wields great authority granted by the Bajoran council of Vedeks.

The first 48 episodes of DEEP SPACE NINE only occasionally explored the main characters in substantial ways. Followers of STAR TREK—THE NEXT GENERATION note that series didn't begin such explorations until season three. Once the setting and background of DEEP SPACE NINE become firmly established, time will be taken to explore the characters.

ORIGINS OF DEEP SPACE NINE

DEEP SPACE NINE is about new frontiers in STAR TREK. They are just beginning to be explored. When the wormhole was discovered near Bajor, this opened the Gamma Quadrant for exploration. Previously, this region of space took 70 years to reach by starship. Now it takes seconds.

After Rick Berman and Michael Piller developed the basic premise for DEEP SPACE NINE in 1991, they used elements from NEXT GENERATION's fifth season episode, "Ensign Ro," as their backdrop. That episode introduced the Bajorans, a refugee people whose homeworld had been conquered by the brutal Cardassians.

Originally Ensign Ro Laren was to be a regular on DEEP SPACE NINE. Unfortunately, the actress, Michelle Forbes, wasn't interested. She believed her recent feature film, KALIFORNIA, would lead to bigger things. The film was a critical and box office failure and her character, although major in that film, was badly underwritten.

The Cardassians were first introduced in the NEXT GENERATION episode "The Wounded." They were elevated to key players in DEEP SPACE NINE. Paramount chose to reveal more about them on STAR TREK—THE NEXT GENERATION so that when they assumed a dominant role in DEEP SPACE NINE their culture and menace would already be established.

BEGINNINGS

As DEEP SPACE NINE opened, the Cardassians had just ended their long occupation of Bajor. When the Cardassians left, Bajor had little left of value. It was left defenseless, and so turned to the Federation.

Bajor applied for membership and requested aid in rebuilding. The Federation agreed.

Some factions on Bajor fear new masters. Commander Sisko maintains a hands-off policy towards Bajoran internal affairs. He hopes to reassure the Bajorans of the Federation's good intentions.

The Cardassians were first introduced in the TNG episode "The Wounded," and slightly amplified in "Ensign Ro." "Chain of Command," a two-part storyline, elevates them to the forefront of the STAR TREK universe.

They capture and torture Jean-Luc Picard on screen, and suddenly become far more dangerous than the Romulans.

From its introduction, there were rumors DEEP SPACE NINE would replace THE NEXT GENERATION. Initially Michael Piller discounted those rumors. The last original episode of STAR TREK—THE NEXT GENERATION was aired in syndication a year and a half after DEEP SPACE NINE premiered. The two hour finale scored higher ratings than anything on ABC, NBC, CBS, or the Fox network.

The crew of the new Enterprise will now advance in rank and the cast will become motion picture stars. THE NEXT GENERATION television series is a 178 episode package of memories.

THE CREATORS

Rick Berman and Michael Piller came to DEEP SPACE NINE as veterans of STAR TREK—THE NEXT GENERA-

TION following the departure of creator Gene Roddenberry.

Piller started in television as a fact-checker for docudramas. Later he worked on the writing staff of MIAMI VICE and SIMON AND SIMON. Many writers want to produce to protect their scripts from rewriting. Piller was no different.

While working on the short-lived series HARD TIME ON PLANET EARTH, he became acquainted with producer Maurice Hurley. Hurley introduced him to Gene R o d d e n b e r r y . Roddenberry invited him to write an episode of THE NEXT GENERATION.

When Maurice Hurley left THE NEXT GENERATION, Roddenberry asked Piller to replace him. He gave Piller a crash course in the STAR TREK universe, educating him in the underlying philosophy of the series. Piller says Roddenberry's influence continues to this day, nearly three years after his death.

Piller co-created DEEP SPACE NINE with Rick Berman. As executive producer, Piller works with the script writers guiding the direction of the series.

Rick Berman oversees day-to-day production of the show. He insures that episodes are shot within deadline and on budget, and supervises editing, post-production, and music.

The series started out to tell the story of a remote space station and the rebuilding of society on the planet it orbits. It became much more with the addition of a new element: a stationary wormhole, the first ever discovered.

This wormhole never changes position at either end. It can be used as a gateway to the distant Gamma Quadrant and its many new worlds and civilizations. Residents of the Gamma Quadrant can also visit Deep Space Nine and Bajor.

RUMBLINGS OF DISCONTENT

DEEP SPACE NINE introduced a new spacecraft, a Runabout. The craft will also appear in the forthcoming series STAR TREK: VOYAGER. A Runabout is a lightly armed, small craft capable of carrying a few passengers.

Another new element is the Maquis, a revolutionary group waging an undeclared war against Cardassians in the demilitarized zone near Bajor. The Maquis quickly grew in importance after the two part episode introducing them in the seventh season NEXT GENERATION episode, "Preemptive Strike."

In the episode, Ensign Ro goes undercover to spy on the Maquis. She then really joins them, again becoming an outlaw from Starfleet.

A year and a half after DEEP SPACE NINE began, the series continues to search for direction. One possibility involves Bajor.

Bajor was introduced as a planet rebuilding itself after regaining independence. The premiere episode, "The Emissary," also introduced the strong religious culture permeating Bajor. A spiritual leader known as the Kai leads the Bajoran people.

When religion mixes with politics, as on Bajor, it causes conflict. When the Kai Opaka, a benevolent religious leader, moved to a planet in the Gamma Quadrant in "Battle Lines," the result was political and religious unrest.

POLITICAL POWER

A new Kai had to be chosen from among the Vedeks, the Bajoran religious leaders. Vedek Bareil was the favorite. The man is honest and upstanding. His rival was Vedek Winn, a woman interested in personal power.

In the second season episode, "The Collaborator," Vedek Winn becomes Kai. Since she has never hidden her distrust of the Federation, trouble lies ahead. Until this interesting story, Vedek Winn had not been seen for nearly 20 episodes. DEEP SPACE NINE is clearly trying new things to build interest.

The wormhole has religious significance to the Bajorans. They believe it was built by the Prophets, the mysterious beings they worship.

Since Sisko communicated with the Prophets, he has been called, "The Emissary." Vedek Winn doesn't let this interfere with her opposition to the Federation. She is concerned with the political consequences of the Federation on her bids for power.

The episode, "Crossover," was DEEP SPACE NINE's version of "Mirror, Mirror." Kira and Bashir discover a parallel universe. Their counterparts on the space station are very different from themselves. Humans occupy a low rung on the ladder.

This episode gave Avery Brooks a rare chance to stretch in an otherwise restrictive role. He plays a conniving Ben Sisko, very unlike the boring version in the normal DEEP SPACE NINE storylines.

CROSSOVERS

The first episode of DEEP SPACE NINE crossed over with THE NEXT GENERATION. The story involves Captain Picard.

Later Dr. Bashir and the space station, but no other characters, appeared in the sixth season NEXT GENERATION episode, "Birthright." The DEEP SPACE NINE connection is a minor element in a story focused on Worf.

Lwaxana Troi, played by Majel Barrett, appeared in the DEEP SPACE NINE episode, "The Forsaken," in the first season. She started playing a dizzy version of Lwaxana, but ended up with a more intelligent character. Audiences have glimpsed this version from time to time, such as in the TNG episode, "Half A Life."

Klingons appeared on DEEP SPACE NINE for the first time in the second season episode, "Blood Oath." They dominate the story.

The three Klingons—Kor, Koloth, and Kang—had appeared in episodes of the original STAR TREK in the 1960s. They were played by the original actors, shifting interest to them even more.

The script valiantly tries to give Dax a critical role, but the colorful Klingons steal every scene. After Dax disobeys orders to go with the Klingons, she encounters no discussion upon her return.

Dax is troubled at killing in battle for the first time. The Klingons are more ready to face the consequences of their attack. The consequences for Dax are never shown.

MORE AND MORE STAR TREKS

DEEP SPACE NINE was created because Paramount wanted to end THE NEXT GENERATION television series after seven seasons. With 178 episodes in the can, the studio could advance the franchise to the big screen and generate more profits. Paramount initially discounted this as a rumor, but many correctly predicted DEEP SPACE NINE would run for the last year and a half of THE NEXT GENERATION before that series concluded.

Fans of NEXT GENERATION wanted the series to continue. Some of the cast of NEXT GENERATION, most notably Marina Sirtis and Jonathan Frakes, express interest in appearing in the fourth STAR TREK series, VOYAGER.

Paramount wants to reserve all NEXT GENERATION actors for the movies. The studio wants to keep the crew intact for feature films, just as the original crew remained together in the six STAR TREK movies.

DEEP SPACE NINE doesn't win the high ratings STAR TREK—THE NEXT GENERATION does. TNG took a couple of years to establish itself in syndication. DEEP SPACE NINE shows signs of growth. The final episodes of the second season explore the characters in new ways.

CARDASSIANS VS THE FEDERATION

The Maquis, an underground group of Federation citizens, stir things up in the demilitarized zone. In the NEXT GENERATION episode, "Preemptive Strike," Cardassians commit crimes against Federation citizens, pushing Ensign Ro to join the Maquis. In the original two-part storyline of DEEP SPACE NINE, "The Maquis," the rebels are portrayed as paranoids. This may not be the case.

In the DEEP SPACE NINE episode, "Tribunal," the Cardassians frame Miles O'Brien for a crime he did not commit to prove Federation complicity with the Maquis. Their plan is to force the Federation to disband their colonies in the demilitarized zone.

Only the discovery of a Cardassian spy engineering the incident prevents it from succeeding. The episode shows the Cardassians are afraid of the Maquis.

Both sides fuel this border war. Colonists attack Cardassian ships and Cardassians attack unarmed colonists. Each side hates the other. While the Maquis lack the official support of the Federation, the Cardassians give full support to their people.

The reach of the Maquis is great. They have unofficial sympathizers in the upper ranks of the Federation.

FACING THE FUTURE

The final episode of year two of DEEP SPACE NINE, "The Dominion," introduces an alien race from the Gamma Quadrant never before seen. They were first mentioned in "Sanctuary" and again in "Rules of Acquisition" by people from the Gamma Quadrant. Nothing about the Dominion was shown until now. The Dominion may become the major antagonist on STAR TREK: VOYAGER.

The second season of DEEP SPACE NINE most often focuses on Miles O'Brien. One episode is told entirely from his point of view. It turns out to be a clone.

In "Tribunal," O'Brien is put on trial in a version of Kafka's "The Trial." He is arrested, imprisoned, and sentenced without knowing his crime. The Cardassians trying O'Brien know he is innocent, but don't care.

Keiko is the most underused character on the series. Although her husband, Miles, is imprisoned by the Cardassians in "Tribunal," she has very few scenes. She's shuttled into the background so Odo can talk to Miles. There are many missed opportunities in this compelling human drama.

The series has become increasingly interesting as time goes by, even if it is very different from STAR TREK—THE NEXT GENERATION.

Successful film series often spawn TV spin-offs. Thus far none have succeeded. ROBOCOP may be the first.

ROBOCOP: THE TV SERIES

The first hit ROBOCOP film created an enduring franchise for Orion Pictures. The second film didn't perform as well. It received a critical drubbing. The third film barely registered at the box office.

None of that mattered. The series was established. Foreign markets wanted more Robo-product.

During the production of the original ROBOCOP film in 1986, co-writer Ed Neumeier discussed the premise of what would turn into a successful series. He said, "This all came out of the fact that I discovered comic books when I was twenty-four. I discovered that there was a new wave of comic books coming out. So it was sort of adolescent, but it was consistently that. Then as we went through subsequent drafts it became a little more sophisticated. The dialogue became more sophisticated."

He continued, "We tried to get motivations for these people instead of just acting out of adolescent rage. I was a story analyst and a reader for five years. I worked as a 'creative executive' on a lot of pictures, but this is the first script I really sat down and wrote since I was in film school at UCLA."

Robocop (Richard Eden) puts the arm on murderous psychopath "Pudface" Morgan (James Kidnie)..

Photo c 1994 Robocop Productions Ltd Partnership

Neumeier was also a producer of the first ROBOCOP. He was able to shape what ROBOCOP would be in all its forms.

"Everything that was done was done with my approval, more or less," he said. "Approval is a funny word because when you're in production and everybody's hysterical, screaming about money, you just go, 'All right, if we can't do this then let's do that.' So my sense of the movie is that it's everything that we could make it, under the circumstances, and it follows my tone and what I wanted to see out of the picture as much as possible. So I'm, on the whole, very happy about it. I think that if you don't like this movie, then you don't like the movie that I set out to write because I think it's very much that."

ORIGINS

Canada's Skyvision Entertainment and Orion Pictures conceived the

ROBOCOP TV series in early 1993. Brian Ross and Kevin Gillis made a deal with Orion to produce a two-hour pilot followed by 21 one-hour episodes. The series would premiere in syndication early in 1994.

The production team for the TV series includes Ross and Gillis as executive producers, and Stephen Downing, formerly executive producer of MacGYVER for seven years. J. Miles Dale produces the show with Bob Wertheimer serving as line-producer.

Downing says, "MacGyver was a similar hero to RoboCop; a loner who fights against injustice, using his wits and humor to get him out of every situation possible."

The non-violent approach taken on MacGYVER intrigued Skyvision. There is now a strong backlash against televised violence. The TV version of RoboCop doesn't rack up a body count. Instead the cyborg finds an appropriate way to take the suspect into custody.

"RoboCop is an Adaptive Cyborg, and as such, has the ability to reason about appropriate force," Downing explains. "He has the judgment and mechanical skill to effectively apply reasonable force in all situations. Through the effect of RoboVision (the computer readout projected on-screen), we can see RoboCop make conscious choices not to use excessive force when alternates exist in a controlled situation."

A THINKING MAN'S ROBOCOP

Violent action filled the original ROBOCOP motion picture. Downing says it doesn't take much effort to stage a shoot-out in which everyone is blown away. He prefers more imaginative solutions to confrontations between RoboCop and the desperadoes.

"I would like to define another kind of hero," Downing adds. "You have to think a little bit to accomplish things in another way. Take for instance in the first movie, that situation where the guy had the Mayor hostage. RoboCop could have just walked in and blown him away, but it was more entertaining to have him use his thermographic vision to locate the guy, reach through the wall and grab him."

The world of ROBOCOP is very different from the contemporary setting of MacGYVER. Downing prepared for the series by immersing himself in Isaac Asimov's robot books. Series star Richard Eden also followed this path. Describing their approach, Downing explains, "Science fiction is a very tight and narrowly defined world. We're trying to be disciplined in our extrapolation of our future. Some people will not like it, some will. If there is a logic to it and it's well-grounded and it's entertaining, then we've got it."

NEW IDEAS FOR THE SERIES

RoboCop still carries his gun in his right leg, but it now has additional capabilities. The producer invented a "tagging" aspect so RoboCop can switch from lethal mode to firing an identification tag.

The gun fires a tiny identification tag encoded with the time of the "tagging" and the officer's name. RoboCop later tracks this tagged person. In the pilot, RoboCop uses the gun to tag his son, Jimmy.

RoboCop's left leg carries devices called S.C.A.D.s, or Suspect Containment Alternative Devices. These devices, introduced in various episodes, include an inflatable balloon that traps people inside a boat or against the wall in a small room. There is also a bolo gun that whips around a fleeing person's legs and trips them.

Instead of Lewis, Murphy now teams with Officer Lisa Madigan. She thinks and acts very much like Lewis. The desk sergeant is now Stan Parks, played by Blu Mankuma. The people of Old Detroit include Gadget, played by Sarah Campbell. She is a little girl who becomes RoboCop's unofficial sidekick and figures in many stories.

Cliff DeYoung plays mad scientist Dr. Cray Z. Millardo in the pilot. He is a brilliant but evil man who develops a supercomputer that requires a living human brain.

When the brains of murdered, homeless men don't work, Cray kills his own secretary. She supplies the final active element for his scheme. The computer controls all of Delta City, and obeys only Dr. Millardo.

This concept originated with a discarded script Neumeier and Miner wrote as a sequel to the first ROBOCOP film. Diana, played by Andrea Roth, is Millardo's secretary. She joins with the computer and develops unforeseen powers. Her mind manifests a hologram of her former body to help RoboCop defeat Millardo.

ON LOCATION IN CANADA

Many syndicated TV shows, including KUNG FU: THE LEGEND CONTINUES, film in Canada. ROBOCOP films in Toronto.

The series began shooting in October 1993 and premiered in March 1994. The pilot completed filming in November at a cost of $5 million. Much of that cost was for sets and costumes that will continue to be used in the series.

The pilot was shot in 24 days of main unit and 12 days of second unit. The normal one-hour episodes are shot on an 8 day schedule, the standard for most one-hour dramas.

Ed Neumeier and Michael Miner scripted the first film in the series. They are back for the TV series.

The original concept emerged a decade ago when Ed Neumeier met fledgling, filmmaker Michael Miner. Neumeier revealed his idea for a futuristic, BLADE RUNNER setting in which a robot policeman developed human intelligence. Miner loved the idea. The pair began to develop a script.

The original script was optioned by Jonathan

Kaplan and producer Jon Davison for Orion Pictures. When Kaplan pursued other projects, Orion signed Paul Verhoeven as director.

After ROBOCOP became a hit, Miner and Neumeier scripted an unused sequel when Orion went in a different direction. Elements of this sequel appear in the pilot for the television series.

IN THE SHADOW OF DELTA CITY

The setting is still the part of Old Detroit not engulfed by Omni-Consumer Products, the company that created RoboCop. They technically "own" him. He is on permanent loan to the police department.

Old Detroit exists in the shadow of Delta City, the futuristic metropolis that exported all its social problems to Old Detroit. Rampaging crime terrorizes the poor and downtrodden.

Alex Murphy is the slain police officer whose head and torso were used for RoboCop. He is actually a cyborg. The human part of him is kept secret outside of Omni-Consumer Products and the Old Detroit police department.

The TV series picks up the human thread of RoboCop's life unwisely jettisoned in the second and third films. Alex Murphy remembers who he is but doesn't burden his wife and son with his new existence.

RoboCop is fiercely protective of his former family. He guards them even if it means violating orders.

ROBOCOP: THE SERIES takes place two years after the original ROBOCOP film. It ignores some things from the two subsequent motion pictures. Murphy's former partner, Lewis, is not one of the regulars in the TV series.

Producer Stephen Downing, with the support of Miner and Neumeier, chose to ignore the events of ROBOCOP 2 and ROBOCOP 3. In the second film Murphy's family learns he is RoboCop.

Lewis is slain in the third film, and RoboCop declares war on Omni Consumer Products. He also sports a new flying suit. The TV series discards these changes.

BACK TO BASICS

Co-creator Ed Neumeier says, "It goes back to the first one in that the relationship with OCP. The way OCP was cast, was much more the way it was in the first movie. Even though they were sort of bad executives, ultimately the Chairman—the Old Man in the movie; for some arcane legal reason, the Chairman is what he's called now—was a benevolent tyrant. We never got into this kind of world where there's good cops and bad cops and corporate policemen who are hurting homeless people. That seemed to be a little too sticky for what is essentially a cop show. That's never been very interesting to me."

Neumeier and Miner initially weren't contacted by the producers. The production company wasn't aware the writing duo had the right of first refusal to write any ROBOCOP TV pilot. When they read about the announced series, they contacted the producers and they had a meeting of the minds.

Says Miner, "We always felt RoboCop was a lonely hero who could not express who he is. The television series is an opportunity to explore the ethical honing of RoboCop's character against a more science fiction-like setting."

Neumeier adds, "ROBOCOP is also a comedy, a social satire in the broadest sense. We were always thinking about the next crazy character, place name, or situation which would pillory our existing institutions."

Neumeier says ROBO-COP takes place at the time of the second industrial revolution. He believes we are just starting to enter this stage of the world's cultural evolution.

ENTER— RICHARD EDEN

Richard Eden, the new Alex Murphy/RoboCop, only appears on-screen during the credits sequence which shows Robo's origin. In the series, whenever RoboCop's helmet is removed, he looks like Peter Weller.

Eden likes playing RoboCop. He added his own touch to the character in the pilot.

He says, "We have a line that I contributed and Stephen Downing was kind enough to allow in—'Images are all that's left of what I was. I want to remember.' That's where he's starting from. He realizes that he cannot be with his family any more but he will be able to protect them from afar. I'm hoping the final thing the audience gets is that Murphy has accepted his destiny, and it's not a bad one at that. Now, if he can only make it work."

RoboCop has become a symbol of hope for humanity because of his unselfishness. Eden adds, "He's not just a machine; but a man, compelled to do the right thing, all the time, by virtue of Alex Murphy's character."

The actor explains, "It's like waking up one morning to discover you're a quadriplegic. They've put on metal arms and so on, but you know you'll never be able to make love again, be touched and held in a normal way again, but you have memories of all that!"

Eden feels that Murphy has become incorruptible. He can no longer derive any benefit from material possessions.

Richard Eden is the third actor to don the Robo-suit. His early work began as a student of the American Academy of Dramatic Arts. He distinguished himself on the stage and earned a Drama Logue Performance Award for his performance of Henry in the play "The Fox." Richard also received an L.A. Critics Circle Award nomination, and a Drama Logue Performance Award for his performance as Stanley Kowalski in "A Streetcar Named Desire."

The actor previously appeared in the daytime

drama SEARCH FOR TOMORROW and on the CBS latenight show FOREVER KNIGHT. Canadian born Eden had a recurring role in the series SANTA BARBARA where he garnered an Emmy Award nomination for Best Supporting Actor. Other television credits include guest shots on FALCON CREST, ST. ELSEWHERE, EMERALD POINT, COUNTERSTRIKE, and SECRET SERVICE.

His feature film work includes appearances in such little seen fare as S H O O T F I G H T E R, OTHER PEOPLE'S MONEY, CLUB FED, SOLAR CRISIS, and CRIME TASK FORCE.

Eden loves his role as RoboCop. He says, "It's wonderful; great! Along with my role in the theatre as Stanley, in 'A Streetcar Named Desire,' it's the most challenging role of my career."

Although Eden previously had little interest in science fiction, his new role caused him to read Isaac Asimov's robot books. Asimov's Three Laws of Robotics pioneered impor-

tant concepts in robotics. Beginning with the first ROBOCOP motion picture, RoboCop had "three prime directives" that governed his behavior. These are 1) To serve the public trust; 2) To protect the innocent; and, 3) To uphold the law. Some forget the secret fourth directive, to harm no one who worked for OCP.

Robovision displays options on RoboCop's internal screen. These form his escalating use-of-force criteria. The list runs from willing compliance to pain compliance to deadly force.

The producers of the TV series don't rule out RoboCop killing someone. If it happens, it will be for a very good reason not casually as in the motion pictures.

ROBO-SPEECH

The cyborg RoboCop speaks like a robot. He doesn't have the casual cadence of human speech. When RoboCop forces someone to comply with a demand to come along, he states: "Thank you for your cooperation."

In describing how he thinks, Eden observes that when Alex Murphy transformed into RoboCop, they took "his right brain functions away and replaced them with that hard drive computer. That means no imagination, just logic, and perhaps some feeling."

They may have also taken away his ability to generate an original idea, but this is not the way Eden sees it. "He is a man. If we were completely logical, like Mr. Spock, we would be extreme," the actor says. "This is like combining Kirk and Spock because you've got the passion and humanity of Alex Murphy and the pure logic and brilliance of RoboCop, and one cannot work without the other.

"I see it as a unity," the actor continues, "the uncommon man. He will adapt and say, 'I will make this work,' instead of blowing his brains out. I'm the sort of actor who loves unpredictability. I hope they take it in that direction, where there are moments when he just wants to yell, 'Let me out of here,' like a lone wolf."

DIFFERENT FEMALE CO-STARS

RoboCop's friend, Officer Lisa Madigan, is played by Yvette Nipar. She appeared in recurring roles on 21 JUMP STREET and the ADVENTURES OF BRISCO COUNTY JR. Lisa also made guest appearances on THE FLASH, BOYS OF TWILIGHT, MURDER SHE WROTE, MIDNIGHT CALLER, MATLOCK, HARDBALL, FULL HOUSE, and THE HUMAN TARGET. Yvette Nipar has appeared in a few little seen feature films including SKI PATROL, TERMINAL ENTRY, RUN IF YOU CAN, and DR. MORDRED.

Describing her character, Officer Lisa Madigan, Nipar says, "I like the 'skin' of her character—she is feisty and determined, and has chosen a career for herself and made it happen. She is very much a modern woman, with her own mind and standards."

The new Roboseries introduced a super computer that manifests itself as a hologram. The hologram takes the form of the woman whose brain powers the machine. Like RoboCop, she, too, has been changed from a human being into a machine.

THE GHOST IN THE MACHINE

Andrea Roth portrays Diana Powers, a woman killed in the pilot episode and resurrected as a hologram. She is the ghost in the machine; a cybernetic entity that takes transparent human form by employing an energy field.

Andrea previously appeared in a number of roles, including guest appearances on MURDER SHE WROTE, HIGHLANDER, FOREVER KNIGHT, PARKER LEWIS CAN'T LOSE, COUNTERSTRIKE, SECRET SERVICE, DANGEROUS CURVES, JACK OF HEARTS, SWEATING

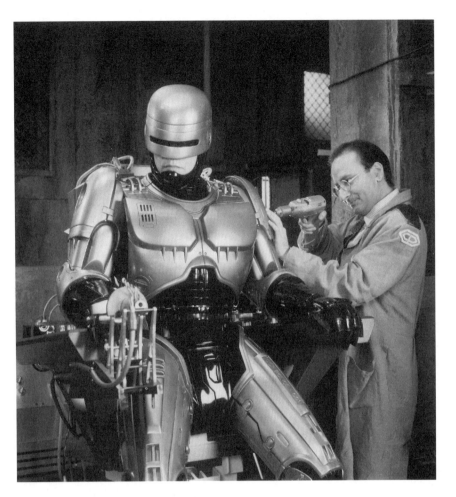

Chief technician Charlie Lippencott (Ed Sahely) gives Robocop (Richard Eden) a tune-up.

BULLETS, ALFRED HITCHCOCK PRESENTS, and, in a regular role, the Canadian series E.N.G.. She most recently played in the Hallmark Hall of Fame special SPOILS OF WAR.

Andrea Roth says, "Only three people know of Diana's existence within the Neuro-Brain computer: her killer Mallardo, RoboCop, and the Chairman. She's a character shrouded in mystery. I also like the juxtaposition between her introduction as a kind of Judy Holliday-like personality at OCP, and her transformation into a powerful, beautiful woman. Diana is fulfilled in life as the Neuro-Brain, because she is now empowered to contribute to a better way of life for thousands-upon-thousands of people."

Diana Powers appears only as a special effect. Andrea does all of her acting in front of a blue screen. Her character is later composited with the film of other characters she interacts with. "I never really know what my final scenes will look like, and it is a challenge to create my own reality around the scripts," Andrea explains.

GADGET AND SGT. PARKS

The other female regular is Sarah Campbell as Gadget. Although only twelve, this young actress already has a variety of credits. She had important roles in WAR OF THE WORLDS, FAMILY PICTURES, THE HIDDEN ROOM, I'LL NEVER GET TO HEAVEN, and DOUBLE STANDARD. She also appeared in the feature films CHANGE OF HEART and BODY PARTS.

Gadget first appeared in the TV pilot. She is the unofficial mascot for Metro South, the police station in Old Detroit.

Sgt. Stan Parks adopts Gadget at the conclusion of the pilot. "I love the storyline with Gadget, and the reluctant father role that is thrust upon Parks," the actor says. "We have a lot of fun with the interaction between Sarah Campbell and myself. I also see Parks as the father of all the cops he sends out on the beat. He cares deeply about their safety."

Blu Mankuma plays Sgt. Stan Parks. The actor, a Seattle native, relocated to Canada during the Vietnam war. He has lived in Vancouver ever since.

Mankuma has appeared in a number of feature films. These include THE RUSSIA HOUSE, BIRD ON A WIRE, STAKEOUT II, LOOK WHO'S TALKING, SHOOT TO KILL, and EUREKA.

On television he's appeared in such TV movies as FOR THE LOVE OF AARON, THE RED SPIDER, BODY OF EVIDENCE, THE GIRL WHO SPELLED FREEDOM, and BROTHERLY LOVE. He's also been in episodes of 21 JUMP STREET, STREET JUSTICE, THE HAT SQUAD, WISEGUY, MacGYVER, and DAVY CROCKETT.

"This role is a great opportunity for me," Makuma explains. "Parks isn't just a traffic cop for all the characters around him; he plays opposite all the series leads. He is a catalyst for much of the human interest in the show."

The role is significant because sergeant is the highest rank at Metro South police department. Above that are only OCP executives issuing conflicting directives to the police department they own and operate.

THE CHAIRMAN OF OCP

David Gardner portrays the Chairman of OmniConsumer Products. This role is equivalent to that of "the Old Man" in the original ROBOCOP movie.

A native Canadian, Gardner has appeared in the films THE GOOD MOTHER, HEARTSOUNDS, THE CLASS OF 1984, IF YOU COULD SEE WHAT I HEAR, PROM NIGHT, WHO HAS SEEN THE WIND, and SPECIAL PEOPLE. Gardner had regular roles on the TV series HOME FIRES and STREET LEGAL, and appeared as a guest star on such series as E.N.G., COUNTERSTRIKE, MY

SECRET IDENTITY, ALFRED HITCHCOCK PRESENTS, WAR OF THE WORLDS, CAPTAIN POWER, NIGHT HEAT, and Canadian TV series.

Gardner plays his role with sensitivity and insight. The Chairman is not a typical evil corporate bureaucrat such as "the Old Man" in ROBOCOP II.

Nancy Murphy is a recurring character not in every episode. She is Alex Murphy's "widow," portrayed by Jennifer Griffin.

Murphy's son, Jimmy, also appears with some regularity. He's played by Peter Costigan.

Murphy learned that even though he spared his family the grief of knowing he is now a cyborg, their problems are far from over. Jimmy sometimes falls victim to the gangs of Old Detroit. A bureaucratic foul-up prevented Nancy Murphy from getting her husband's police pension, so they end up on welfare.

RoboCop finds this intolerable. Nancy meets RoboCop in Old Detroit more than once, but remains unaware he is her husband.

DRAMATIC DEPARTURES

Detective Lisa Madigan, Murphy's former partner, knows the secret pain Murphy feels. She helps keep an eye on Nancy and Jimmy, but honors Alex's request not to reveal the truth.

The TV series stresses action, satire, and humanity, hallmarks of the first film. The original film balanced a very dark look at the future with TV blackouts. These have continued in ROBOCOP: THE FUTURE OF LAW ENFORCEMENT. MediaBreak newsbits include cartoon segments featuring Commander Cash. They are imaginative and darkly satirical.

Commander Cash, the on-air spokesman for OmniConsumer Products, was created by animation writers Pamela Hickey and Dennys McCoy. Along with writer Joe Pearson, they reinterpreted the character for ROBOCOP.

"Recognizing the potential for Commander Cash was immediate," Executive Producer Kevin Gillis recalls. "My background is in music and animation, and when I read the Commander Cash outlines, I knew we had to have him animated."

Nelvana Productions, a Canadian animation company, creates the animation. Commander Cash appears in each episode of ROBOCOP with messages about the fantastic things OCP can provide

THE ALEX MURPHY QUESTION

The original ROBOCOP introduced the concept of a man merged with a machine. The film explored the cyborg's impact on the people who know RoboCop and the people who knew Alex Murphy. The human element is very strong in the TV series.

"The shining humanity of RoboCop is the recurring theme of this show,"

Eden stresses. "We have a responsibility to let Alex Murphy show through the suit."

Murphy's humanity finds anchor in memories of his wife and son. He still loves them unselfishly. He refuses to reveal he became a cyborg because he feels they will not accept the change.

Says Murphy, "I cannot be with them, but I can protect them."

Murphy remembers who he is, so OCP cannot use him like a soulless machine to do their bidding. He refuses guidance from the greedy, misguided people who created him.

ALTERNATIVES TO VIOLENCE

The ROBOCOP TV series stresses imagination over violence. RoboCop never kills. He only shoots to wound.

The violence of the original ROBOCOP film was not a necessary element. This was proven when a heavily edited version aired on network TV a few years ago. It held up extremely well on the strength of story and characters.

The gun on the TV series is a lighter version of the one in the first movie. The original was a 9mm weapon. They created a lighter gun when importing the real gun into Canada proved difficult. It is easier to handle by the actor in the Robo-suit.

The series films in Canada for around $1.25 million per episode. Canadian productions have come a long way since WAR OF THE WORLDS, RAY BRADBURY THEATER, and AIRWOLF. Shows currently produced in Canada such as ROBOCOP and KUNG FU: THE LEGEND CONTINUES demonstrate high production values and expertise in execution of action and cinematography.

DESIGNING THE FUTURE

Ten series scripts were ready for production when principal photography ended on the pilot. This gave other departments, such as the designers and the futurists, time to do their best work.

"ROBOCOP is the culmination of a multitude of people and departments," Line Producer Bob Wertheimer explains. "The series is shot on 35mm film and conformed to tape. The production utilizes blue screen and special effects, matte paintings, traditional and computer animation, and stunt performances. We deliver on-time, and on-budget."

Cinespace studios in Toronto devotes fifty thousand square feet of permanent sets to simulate Old Detroit and its environs, including OmniConsumer Products headquarters. Production Designer Perri Gorrara says, "The design of the series is not totally futuristic—rather a blend of very old and the newest techno-chrome, that can be designed and delivered to our near future world."

Large matte paintings created by John Fraser generate the illusion of Delta City's daylight and night-time settings. A huge blue screen hangs from the rafters outside the window of the set for the office and boardroom of The Chairman. These paintings represent a merging of skylines of the present and future Detroit with the existing skyline of Toronto.

For some of the buildings, Fraser took Perri Gorrara's set designs and built miniature skyscrapers around the individual set. The entire city exists in computer files. Inputting specific lens and location information creates and enhances any point of view.

The series uses special effects only to enhance a script. "It's not the effects, it's the story," visual effects supervisor Lee Wilson points out.

SHAPING THE FUTURE

"Every visual aspect of the show receives careful consideration as to its look and utility," says Gorrara. Entire cottage industries have sprung up in Toronto to meet the demand for tooling and production of the props and accessories that represent the future.

The first RoboCop film employed futuristic looking cars. The Ford Motor Company has supplied the TV series with a special 1994, 5-Litre Ford Mustang prototype. The Detroit Police force employs twenty additional Ford automobiles in the TV series. Other vehicles include two Hummers from the AM General Corporation and the Orion II, an urban transport for the disabled supplied by Ontario Bus Industries. All have been painted and fitted with a high-tech skin representing near future technology, including state-of-the-art emergency roof lighting.

The TV ROBOCOP emphasizes science fantasy more than the films did. The series introduced Diana Powers as the dead woman resurrected inside a super-computer.

Other examples include villains such as Pudface Morgan, portrayed by James Kidnie. Unfortunately this character is completely over the top. His make-up makes Pudface look like Freddy Krueger.

ROBOCOP takes place in the 21st Century. No specific date is given in the series, but it could easily be near 2018, the same year in which SEAQUEST DSV takes place.

Confederations run the world of SEAQUEST, while information networks run industrial blocs and global political institutions in the world of ROBOCOP. The corporations are all powerful. Society comes in a distant second.

THE WORST OF TODAY

The beginning of each episode says the stories take place in the "Near Future." Downing explains, "The near-future genre is always dark by necessity, because it's always an extrapolation of the worst of today."

The first ROBOCOP film hurls satirical barbs at corporations and the drones who control them. This element also appears in the TV series.

Alex Murphy is a victim of the corporate system since the thugs who kill him secretly work for OmniCorp. He is also its s p o k e s m a n . OmniConsumer Products (OCP) resurrects Murphy and turns him into RoboCop, prototype of a line hailed as "The future of law enforcement."

RoboCop is a cyborg. A powerful casing with robotic arms and legs contains remains of Murphy's human body. The Chairman of OCP emerges as RoboCop's surrogate father, protecting the new entity.

Production designer Perri Gorrara has her own vision of RoboCop. She says, "I see RoboCop as a modern medieval knight. His augmentation is equivalent to armor; his home in the basement of Metro South, is like a dungeon or Keep. His chair, a throne for a noble man. He rides out into the surrounding countryside to do battle with the forces of evil. I think it is all rather romantic!"

DELTA CITY AND OLD DETROIT

Delta City was still on the drawing boards in the original ROBOCOP motion picture. It now towers over the decaying husk of Old Detroit.

Delta City is just what OCP wants it to be. After its construction, OCP turned their backs on Old Detroit, allowing rogue elements to run wild. The police department is underfunded and under-manned.

OCP focuses on the future, represented by Delta City. The decaying metropolis of Old Detroit represents failed experiments of the past. Poverty exists in the shadow of opulence, just as it does in many modern cities of the 1990s.

The police headquarters of Old Detroit, Metro South, represents a crossover between old and new, past and future. Alex Murphy, RoboCop, works at Old South, as does Sgt. Stan Parks. Old desks and filing cabinets crammed with papers stand side by side with modern computer equipment. The basement contains a state of the art lab where scientist maintenance man Charlie Lippencott services RoboCop.

Production designer Perri Gorrara believes this combination of old and new makes perfect sense. "In life," he says, "we tend to drag what is functional along with us instead of creating a totally new environment."

The wide-angle look of the series cinematography moves beyond the limitations of normal sets and sound stages. Gorrara continues, "Our sets must be complete, functioning rooms with ceilings in place and dressed for reality. The ceilings break away for over-head shots, yet often we will drop the camera to accentuate the stature of RoboCop in a scene. We have the flexibility to accommodate every camera angle."

The series nine standing sets are large and detailed. They include a wall of video monitors inside the offices of OCP and a blue screen facility outside the office windows to simulate day and night scenes on the set. Three other sets stand in for warehouses and other locales in Old Detroit or Delta City.

ENTER THE VIDEO TOASTER

Gorrara explains that many episodes employ inventions of the scriptwriter's imagination. He says, "We design all of the gadgetry on the show in house, and that is a challenge. We research the feasibility of such a device existing and then build upon known devices which will likely evolve into the ultra-new weapon or communications device. It doesn't stop there; we also have to think of what the next microwave equivalent will look like and design and build it."

The special visual effects for ROBOCOP are created in-house and not sub-contracted to other companies as with most TV series. Visual Effects Supervisor Lee Wilson explains, "In-house we used a Video Toaster system, which won an Emmy Award for advancing television technology [the same system employed by BABYLON 5], and the Amiga 4000 computer."

Ann-imation Video Special Effects uses the SGI system for sub-contract work on ROBOCOP. "The combination of the two systems incorporates all of the elements of visual and special effects design and computer animation with live action against blue screen and mattes, creating an exciting and totally unique look," he explains.

The production crew considers Diana the crowning achievement of their visual effects. Says writer and co-producer John Sheppard, "She is so beautiful, truly living up to the script description: goddess-like."

Diana's energy field and three-dimensional materializations and dematerializations add to the reality of the character.

The Visual Effects Department is also responsible for computer readouts on the monitors in the RoboCruiser and those seen in the Metro South squad room and other locales. They create the computer imaging for RoboCop's visor. They also created the backgrounds for Diana's trip through RoboCop's neuro-nets.

SPECIAL STREET EFFECTS

Other special effects for ROBOCOP involve stunt-work by special effects experts performed by a team under the supervision of Michael Kavanagh. In the climax of the TV pilot, effects include burning cars, explosions, and fight scenes. Stunt men wearing roller blades and riding motorcycles hurl through the air while RoboCop lays siege to the barricaded Public Works building.

They accomplished this in a variety of ways. The cars are empty shells stripped of tires, seats, and engines to remove all combustibles. There was no danger of explosion. The cars were set on fire with black powder and spark charges.

The Emergency Task Force (ETF) division of the Toronto Metropolitan Police Force works with the production team to co-ordinate filming on city streets for explosions, rollovers, and chase scenes. Safety is paramount.

Before stunts are done on location, they are tested on the back-lot of the studio. These trial runs are recorded on video.

Second unit director T.J. Scott explains, "There is a lot on-going on this show. My background is in stunt performance and I have worked on many big budget films, but I have never seen anything on this scale in television."

The 90 pound RoboCop suit restricts the movement of the actor or stunt man wearing it. The mask restricts vision. This makes stunt work more difficult.

The series uses three different fiberglass Robo-suits. They are heavily insured against theft or damage. Without the suits, the show can't go on.

ROBO-STUNTS

Stunt co-ordinator Larry McClean explains, "Making the stunts look seamless requires the co-operation of all parties on the set. Within a scene we have sparks, representing gunshots, deflecting off of

RoboCop's armor plating, explosions from high tech weaponry, stunt falls, fights and the actor's performance to coordinate with the first and second unit directors."

The stunts are often wild and comedic. They require creativity to make them interesting on screen. One recent stunt involved a wrecking ball coming through the wall with RoboCop grabbing onto it as it swings out from the building and over the street.

To simulate bullets bouncing off RoboCop's armor, the stunt double, Ken Quinn, dons the Robo-suit. Then a special air gun fires round gelcaps which ignite and make a spark as they hit the suit. The gelcaps don't follow a precise trajectory. They sometimes hit the stunt man in unprotected areas.

Another part of the special effects crew makes the prosthetics for Richard Eden's face when RoboCop's mask is removed. Gordon Smith supervises this work.

It takes three hours to apply the full face silicon mask to the actor. The actor explains, "That's glued onto my face, along with the entire mechanism that goes around my head."

THE ROBO-SUIT

Rob Bottin designed The RoboCop armor for the original motion picture. Dennis Pawlik and his "RoboTeam" maintain the new, lighter weight version

The five versions of the RoboCop armor vary in range of movement. Suit adjustments in an action environment involve careful attention to detail by Pawlik. Some Robosuits simulate damage from fire or gunshots.

"The movement of RoboCop is best defined as subtle," Richard Eden explains. "The choreographed movement must look real in a situation." Stunt double Ken Quinn adds, "The stunt Robo-suit is padded and articulated to allow me a free range of movement and yet take a fall. It's a tricky piece of business. If not carefully coordinated, the suit itself can hurt you in an uncontrolled environment."

One day during filming, Eden tripped and fell while

wearing the Robo-suit. Some cables hadn't been moved from his path, the helmet visor obscured his vision, and down he went.

"Thank God it was grass," the actor recalls, "but there you are, going down with 90-odd pounds of Fiberglas on and there's nothing you can say except, 'shi-i-i-i-t,' like Butch Cassidy and the Sundance Kid when they went off the cliff. I bang into lights that I don't see; stuff like that. It's really quite undignified and ungraceful. I think I'm going to need a seeing-eye Robodog to follow me around."

There is a shiny, attractive version of the suit dubbed "GQ." It is used for posed shots for publicity photos.

The armor makes clickety-clack noises when the actor moves. They add the suit's motor noises after filming and eliminate the ambient noises from the soundtrack.

INSIDE ALEX MURPHY

Richard Eden discussed what he'd like to see the ROBOCOP series accomplish. He refers to the first movie as the most human of the three motion pictures, saying, "I believe in more humanity and less heroics. The producers want the opposite, so I think between the two of us, we're going to have a wonderful character."

The two hour premiere reestablishes the original movie while toning down the violence and brutality. The pilot continues the ideas of the first film while introducing new supporting characters.

MODERN MARVELS?

The original ROBOCOP introduces two nitwit news anchors on "Newsbreak"— "You give us three minutes, we'll give you the world." They report on events effecting the story about to appear.

Commander Cash is a new addition for TV. He is a satirical animated segment ostensibly promoting the products of OCP. The products and ideals he promotes are so wacky one can only hope this isn't the real future.

One episode features a "Pet Recycler." A Commander Cash spot shows a child's pet cat run over by a car. When she begins to cry, Commander Cash demonstrates how the cat's remains can be recycled in a container. The remains are then recycled into pet food!

The early episode "Prime Suspect" features an evangelist, Reverend Bob. He stirs up a small group that deems RoboCop an abomination. This episode mentions a company called Cybertek that wants to create more RoboCops using the cryogenically frozen remains of the "Cryovets." It doesn't happen, but it shows the idea of creating more cyborgs is still under serious consideration.

A new element introduced in the series explains why no more RoboCops were created. It seems no one knows why RoboCop works! Previous experiments failed. RoboCop is the only success, but no one knows why. The only way to find out would be to disassemble him.

FRAMED FOR MURDER

"Prime Suspect" explores the human side of RoboCop.

When an evangelist calls him soulless, Robo attends church to decide whether he still has a human soul. Diana Powers tries to soothe his concerns, observing, "I will never know why so many people think that God speaks to us through loudmouth jerks."

When RoboCop is framed for the murder of Reverend Bob, one of the Newsbreak anchors breaks the story with the sound bite, "Say it ain't so, Robo."

Throwaway bits appear in each show. Robo and Officer Madigan enter a closed church in which Alex Murphy had been married years before. According to Madigan it's closed due to the Vatican bank crash mentioned but never referred to again.

This is a good, typical episode of ROBOCOP. It presents an interesting story filled with references to future life in Delta City and Old Detroit. They help create an interesting and imaginative backdrop that adds texture to the story.

"Trouble In Delta City" parodies diet fads. A product introduced by OCP called "NoGain" is an effective but

THE NEW SCI FI TV BOOK

addictive diet pill. One side effect robs a person of all sense of right and wrong. This was the OCP product sabotaged by Dr. Cray Z. Mallardo shortly before his capture.

TROUBLE IN DELTA CITY

Every episode opens with an on-screen statement that reads: "Time: The Near Future." This places the series near 2018, also the time of SEAQUEST DSV.

A "Newsbreak" in this episode reveals that Old Detroit suffered "only 312 murders" in the previous month, a 5% drop from the norm. The grinning newscasters try to convince viewers that this is good news.

When RoboCop encounters Alex Murphy's wife, he quickly excuses himself, explaining, "Excuse me, I have to go. Somewhere there is a crime happening." This line appears in other episodes in similar situations.

Commander Cash returns in "Trouble In Delta City." The segment extols the virtues of pollution. He explains that pollution is "A natural bi-product of prosperity and progress."

He also points out, "The Anti-Pollution industry—where would they be without pollution?" The satire of ROBOCOP explores familiar contemporary issues.

THE HUMAN ADVENTURE

The best episodes include a strong human element in familiar settings, such as when a mad bomber attacks OCP installations. The bomber, Felix Webber, is a balding man with a huge black widow spider tattooed on his forehead. He hates OCP because they canceled his experimental program before he could find a cure for baldness with a hair growth serum distilled from spider venom.

Enter Russell Murphy, Alex Murphy's father, a retired policeman played by Martin Milner. One great scene puts RoboCop in Russell's home. The mother and father of Alex Murphy don't know their son is alive and standing before them in the RoboCop armor.

Robo looks at a family portrait of Alex, his wife, and their newborn baby. When Alex's mother walks up to him, he turns, looks at her, and says, "I am sorry about your loss."

For just an instant, when he says, "I am. . .," the audience believes he might reveal who he really is. It's a tense and touching moment.

This excellent character driven episode teams Russell Murphy with RoboCop when Felix Webber escapes from jail and goes on a new bombing rampage. Russell was the officer in charge during Webber's last bombing spree.

Stewart Granger, the leader of a SWAT team, thinks Russell Murphy is an old timer getting in the way. Granger is portrayed as an excessively officious cartoon, an interesting contrast to the subtle interplay between RoboCop and his father. Of course, Russell Murphy never discovers Robo is his son.

INSIDE OLD DETROIT

Character development highlights this series. The positive portrayal of RoboCop offsets the darkness of the stories. In the shadow of the futuristic Delta City, RoboCop and his fellow police officers fight for decency in Old Detroit. They face crime at its worst, especially when enhanced by the latest technological marvels.

The future portrayed on ROBOCOP is dystopic. Society continues to decay. Humor and parody don't make the world more attractive, only more palatable to the viewing audience. While the first ROBOCOP motion picture is wildly imaginative and entertaining, it portrays a sleazy future no one would want any part of. Whether the rest of America and the world is any better than Old Detroit and its environs hasn't been revealed.

This series is a view of the future from a place where things are grimy and not well cared for. RoboCop is clearly needed.

The other side of the coin appears on SEAQUEST DSV. One can easily believe the that glittering world of 2018 may contain places such as Old Detroit. This is what ROBOCOP is all about.

For the first time since AMAZING STORIES ran on TV in the 1980s, Steven Spielberg has a show back on the air. It premiered in the fall of 1993 to mixed reviews but with a determination to succeed.

SEAQUEST: DSV

Outer space is the final frontier in STAR TREK, but Earth's last frontier is the oceans. Water covers four-fifths of the planet's surface yet vast regions of the sea bottom remain unexplored.

For millennium, the siren call of the trackless seas lured writers to stretch their imaginations. The most famous, Jules Verne's 20,000 LEAGUES UNDER THE SEA, offered a super submarine, the Nautilus. Walt Disney turned the classic French novel into a movie in the 1950s. A few years later, Irwin Allen imagined his own futuristic Seaview for VOYAGE TO THE BOTTOM OF THE SEA.

In 1993 Steven Spielberg's Amblin Entertainment produced a series that draws its inspiration more from Irwin Allen than Jules Verne. SEAQUEST DSV chronicles the adventures of a supposedly civilian vessel commissioned by the United Earth/Oceans Organization. The vessel explores the ocean depths of the world.

Although renewed for a second season, the series experienced tough voyaging during its first year. Creative experimentation resulted in different kinds of stories. The show struggles to find its sea legs.

Steven Spielberg is an Executive Producer of SEAQUEST, along with David J. Burke and Patrick Hasburgh. Describing his reasons for the series, Spielberg states, "When I was a kid, one of the movies and books that inspired me more than any other was 20,000 LEAGUES UNDER THE SEA, and I used to pretend to be Captain Nemo and had a lot of undersea adventures with my Nautilus crew. I'd always wanted to explore the possibility of the depths of our oceans, which cover 70% of our planet, as a stage, as a theater for all sorts of drama and science and entertainment."

Spielberg continues, "So along comes Captain Bridger and the Seaquest crew. Now, originally when I thought this could be done as a feature film, and we began to pitch ideas about what the different adventures would be, the adventures were so self-contained with beginnings, middles and ends that it seemed like it would short-change the concept just to have one two-hour movie;

that in fact we could produce 22 hours of single-hour adventures, and really pretty much cover everything we wanted to do.

"SEAQUEST is part science, it's part fiction and it's part complete and pure fantasy. It combines a real scientific basis with imagination and all sorts of inklings into what the future has in store for us. The world underwater is going to provide farming for future generations, and the year 2018 isn't that far away. Neither is the possibility of the 'new frontier,' which perhaps isn't outer space just yet; the 'new frontier' perhaps is under water," he concludes.

THE SPIELBERG TOUCH

Steven Spielberg may be the only producer/director in the world as recognizable as the many actors he made famous. People attend movies on the strength of Spielberg's name. He has directed or produced six of the top 20 box-office champs, including the number one and two slots occupied by

JURASSIC PARK and E.T. THE EXTRA-TERRES-TRIAL.

Spielberg's career began in television in 1969. When he was twentyone, he directed the NIGHT GALLERY TV movie.

He also directed the pilot for COLOMBO and the now legendary TV movie, DUEL. Years later Spielberg discovered that Universal had allowed the producers of the THE INCREDIBLE HULK TV series to use massive amounts of footage from DUEL—and then attach someone else's name as director. They treated DUEL as stock footage. This helped spur Spielberg to join other film-makers encouraging Congress to adopt legislation protecting motion pictures from wholesale tampering.

The genesis of SEAQUEST is difficult to trace. Rockne S. O'Bannon created the series but left before the premiere. His name remains as sole series creator. O'Bannon got his start on television with the NEW TWILIGHT ZONE, and then wrote the movie ALIEN NATION.

The cast of SEAQUEST on NBC.

Photo ©1994 Universal City Studios

Roy Scheider as Capt. Nathan Bridger of the Seaquest.

He had severe "creative differences." The studio production notes now list the casting director and the costume designer, but not the show's creator. The presspack provides no biographical information on O'Bannon, although scientific consultant Dr. Robert Ballard is interviewed at length.

CREATING SEAQUEST

Amblin Entertainment brought in O'Bannon to develop the series based on little more than a desire to do an undersea TV show. "They basically had a three sentence idea of what it would be about," O'Bannon recalls, "a big submarine, and it should take place in the future because no such submarines currently exist."

O'Bannon wrote the series bible. It outlines what it's all about, including the character profiles. He explains it was always their intention to set the series in a recognizable near future. "We're not projecting that in 25 years our world is going to be

Jules Verne cities under the sea," O'Bannon explains. "There are some big colonies under construction, but I think you'll always see those with scaffolding and work going on. You're not going to come down over a rise and see a giant Chicago 1500 feet down. It's not so far off that you draw only the audience that is young and particularly well read and would be interested in speculative fiction."

He continues, "It's basically the year 2018 and it's along the lines, in tone, of what I did with ALIEN NATION, which was just a short jaunt in the future. What's fun is you can do rifts on what it will be like in the 21st century."

The series offers an optimistic view of the future. O'Bannon says, "So many films deal with a future which is polluted and dark and pessimistic. That's not the take we have at all. Man is not retreating to the oceans in order to survive. It's the opposite. Technology has advanced to the point where deep ocean exploration is possible.

"I remember reading a poll taken of high school students and a huge percentage of them felt that there would be some sort of nuclear war or cataclysmic event in their lifetime. You could see if they believed that was so, it makes you far more interested in short term return than knuckling down and getting a good education and planning for the future. I'm hoping this show will give a sense that we are going to be around and it'll actually be an exciting world to live in," he concludes.

CREATIVE DIFFERENCES

Tommy Thompson replaced O'Bannon on the series. He didn't last long.

Reportedly he clashed with series star Roy Scheider over the direction of the show. Thompson wanted character driven stories.

One story he wanted would have put the characters under pressure magnifying their problems by letting them think they were the only people left alive on

Earth. Roy Scheider nixed the downbeat story. Spielberg didn't like it either.

David J. Burke replaced Thompson. He also became an Executive Producer. Burke previously held that title on the WISEGUY series.

Burke started out in television on CRIME STORY. Both WISEGUY and CRIME STORY took chances, keeping the audience on their toes with unusual storylines.

Patrick Hasburgh is the remaining Executive Producer on SEAQUEST. His previous credits include 21 JUMP STREET, THE A-TEAM and HARDCASTLE AND McCORMICK.

Co-Executive Producer Robert Engels worked as story editor on WISEGUY and producer/writer of the quirky, but critically praised, TWIN PEAKS. Another WISEGUY alumnus on SEAQUEST, Les Sheldon, worked as a producer/director for that highly praised series.

They joined to steer the course of SEAQUEST, navigating troubled waters.

The setting of SEAQUEST in 2018 allows many political and technological changes in a still familiar and comfortable world. Nathan Bridger, played by Roy Scheider, invented the super submarine, Seaquest. He withdrew from the project after the death of his son, a military man.

THE SHAPE OF THE WORLD

The world changed in twentyfive years. The New World Order consists of blocks of nations with conflicting interests including the exploitation of the world's oceans. Many undersea colonies specialize in farming, mining or manufacturing.

The Seaquest often lends assistance to colonies in trouble. The Seaquest (or "seaQuest" as publicity materials prefer to spell it) is a DSV, a "deep submergence vehicle," with a variety of missions. It houses a massive laboratory to conduct research at sea.

The Seaquest also patrols the sea lanes as a

military peace keeper. This creates conflict as scientific personnel object to military missions, even though the United Earth/Oceans Organization (UEO) funded the massive project.

Created as a futuristic version of the United Nations, the governments of the world unite in an enforcement body dedicated to peace, the UEO. The Seaquest adds the realm of the ocean floor to the territory of the United Earth/Oceans Organization.

In the first episode the commander of Seaquest is relieved of duty and stripped of her rank after she attempts to start an atomic war. Nathan Bridger reluctantly leaves his remote island hideaway and returns to the Seaquest to help break in the new captain.

Series supporting characters include Stephanie Beacham as Dr. Kristin Westphalen, Stacy Haiduk as Chief Engineer Lt. Commander Katherine Hitchcock, and Ted Raimi as communications officer Lt. Tim O'Neill. Don Franklin plays Commander Jonathan Ford, the second-in-command. Jonathan Brandis, co-star in several motion pictures, plays sixteen year old science wiz Lucas Wolenczak. John D'Aquino plays Lt. Ben Krieg, the appropriations officer. Royce D. Applegate portrays Manilow Crocker, the chief of security. Marco Sanchez appears as sensor chief Miguel Ortiz, who oversees the external probes of the Seaquest.

DARWIN'S SECRETS

The most unusual cast member is the dolphin, Darwin. Nathan Bridger rescued a male bottlenose dolphin tangled in a fishing net near his home on a remote tropical island. He nursed the injured dolphin back to health, while developing a shared vocabulary of one hundred twentyfive words. Sometimes the shared vocabulary seems much larger, as when Darwin translates telepathic messages.

Aboard the Seaquest, a computer developed by Lucas translates Darwin's

SEAQUEST (DSV-4600)

Length: 1007 feet

Beam: 100 feet

Displacement: 31,700 Tons (Submerged)

Propulsion: Nuclear fusion-power turbines (closed system)

Fuel: Tritium (Extracted from seawater)

Accommodations: 232 total—

88 regular Navy operational crew

124 Scientific personnel

20 Non-Regular personnel (I.G.'s—Invited Guests)

Year Design Began: 2007

Year Commissioned: 2013

PRIMARY SPACES ABOARD SHIP

Bridge

Engineering

Central Computer Chamber

EVA/Probe Bays (4)

whistles and clicks into words uttered by a synthesized voice. The voice sounds suspiciously like an imagined dolphin's voice. It sounds just like the dolphin voices used in the 1973 movie THE DAY OF THE DOLPHIN. This supposedly extends contemporary research that translates certain dolphin sounds into human equivalents.

The Seaquest DSV has a mammal port through which Darwin enters and exits. The submarine doesn't restrict the dolphin to a holding tank. A network of water-filled tubes runs the length of the Seaquest behind the bulkheads, exiting at interior pools throughout the vessel. Dr. Robert Ballard, the scientific consultant on the series, finds this idea realistic.

"I used to train dolphins some twenty years ago," he recalls. "I would take them into the ocean and use them as diving buddies. So having a trained dolphin on board the submarine is totally believable. We were working on speech conversion years ago. Some people may have a hard time believing Darwin can speak because they don't know what the reality is. As a person that deals in that world it's very credible and educational."

A real dolphin performs tricks for the series, but a mechanical dolphin creates the more difficult stunts. It also stands-in when the real Darwin becomes fatigued during the long working day at the studio.

Despite audiences savvy to special effects, stand-ins, and filming with animals, Universal refuses to release information on Darwin. The little available information came from two actors unsure whether they should have said as much as they did.

SCHEIDER'S TV PREMIERE

Roy Scheider never appeared in a television series before. The presence of Steven Spielberg as an executive producer persuaded him to join this undertaking.

The producers wanted to be scientifically accurate in portraying undersea adventures. Dr. Robert Ballard came aboard as scientific consultant. Ballard became world famous when his expedition discovered the Titanic and photographed it with mini-submarines.

Scheider researched his character with the help of Dr. Ballard. With Ballard's assistance, Scheider spent a day aboard a nuclear submarine at the Groton naval base in Connecticut. He observed the vessel undergoing battle maneuvers.

Ballard encouraged Scheider and his wife to swim with dolphins at the mammal research center, Dolphins Plus, in Key Largo, Florida. Scheider and other cast members took a tour of the Scripps Institution of Oceanography in La Jolla and Sea World in San Diego.

Episodes of SEAQUEST incorporate Dr. Ballard's photography with new scenes of underwater phenomena created by the special effects department. Ballard's film of an unusual phenomenon called "black smokers" appears in an episode. He filmed the effect at 9,000 feet below sea level.

SEAQUEST IS LAUNCHED

On the strength of the pilot script and additional story premises, NBC ordered 22 episodes for the first season. The network risked a huge commitment as each episode costs $1.3 million dollars.

Traditionally network fees cover most of the cost, but the studio, in this case Universal, makes up the difference. A series operates at a deficit until it produces enough episodes for syndication.

Five huge sound stages at Universal Studios Hollywood provided the site for shooting during the first season. Darwin's set encompasses adjoining twin tanks named Sea Deck and Moonpool. They were built on the massive sound stage 28 at Universal, along with the main bridge set. This sound stage also housed

Sick Bay

Galley

Science Laboratories (17)

Off Duty Lounge

Crew Quarters

EVA ASSETS

Stinger: Attack Vehicles, Seat 1 (11)

Sea Speeders (4)

Virtual Reality Probe

WSKRS ("Whiskers"): Wireless Sea Knowledge Retrieval

Satellites (8)

Sea Launch: 30 personnel, 1.4 Tons Cargo (4)

Crabs: Aquatic and Robotic Undersea Construction Vehicles (12)

the silent PHANTOM OF THE OPERA and some sets from that film still remain.

The sets on Stage 28 make up 20% of the submarine. Other interior sets include the sea-to-surface shuttle, the bridge of a renegade submarine seen in the first episode, a launch bay center, the captain's quarters including his hologram computer display, and other interiors built for only one episode. The last include the sunken but preserved Library of Alexandria, supposedly located in a hidden grotto off the coast of Egypt.

Some exteriors film on the Universal backlot. The Mexican villas and pueblos in the Universal Studios Hollywood tour became the South American village in the Amazonian Confederation.

Beginning with the second season of SEAQUEST DSV, filming shifts to Universal Studios Florida. The relocation will cause minor cast changes.

CAN YOU SEE UNDERSEA?

SEAQUEST was planned as a family show to air in an early Sunday night slot. While the show is visually dazzling, it can not be as violent as other Spielberg films such as GREMLINS, Indiana Jones, or JAWS.

The special effects of SEAQUEST are impressive, although the initial visuals of the submarine are too dark. They rectified this in later episodes.

The underwater craft looks too realistic instead of murky and shapeless. All futuristic undersea craft are computer generated. A "Video Toaster" graphics board on an Amiga computer created these special effects. The two-hour premiere featured seventyfive computer-generated images. Some became stock footage for later episodes, a common procedure on TV series with many special effects.

Special effects generated by the Video Toaster look like traditional models and pyrotechnics. The effects include undersea explosions and spotlights pinpointing objects glimpsed underwater. James Cameron's film THE ABYSS set the standard for deep sea adventure films. Virtually everything since looks like that film.

Many craftsmen contribute to SEAQUEST, including production designer Richard Lewis and art director Jim Lima. Lima also supervises CGI, Computer Generated Imaging. Video monitors on the bridge display information created by a different crew of video operators. They program the screens from behind the scenes.

THE NATURE OF SEAQUEST DSV

The Seaquest, the largest, fastest, most powerful submarine ever conceived possesses an unlimited range. The submarine never needs to surface. Shuttles hurtle between the surface and the ship.

The exterior hull of the Seaquest acts like a living organism. The sub repairs its own outer hull damage.

Traditional submarines employ sonar and periscopes. The Seaquest uses wireless probes that circle the vessel to secure information. The probes display their information to a crew member wearing a hyper-reality helmet and gloves. It creates a virtual reality environment, replicating what the wireless probes detect.

Dr. Ballard says the fictional submarine isn't as fantastic as it seems. He insists, "The planning that's gone into the design of the submarine deals with real situations. It has been carefully thought out. We're not evolving the technology of this show from episode to episode; it's already there, which will make SEAQUEST even more credible. We actually designed a submarine from the keel out, and one that is technologically believable based upon a logical stretch of what we see on the drawing boards today. There is actual use of technology as we portray it to be in 25 years."

He continues, "It's fun using tomorrow's technology. That's the root of my involvement, to make it believable, to obey the laws of physics. For example, the clam-shell doors going into Seaquest are for flooding the submarine or parts of the ship when we go even deeper. We haven't revealed many things about our submarine but we will in subsequent episodes."

The Seaquest enforces the volatile peace recently established among undersea colonies and vessels. Its mission to protect colonies and vessels and lend immediate aid to all sub-surface inhabitants takes priority over its normal role exploring the world beneath the sea.

The ship engages in rescue operations. On one such mission, at the behest of the Amazonian Confederation, it captures a rogue submarine supposedly smuggling emeralds. When the Seaquest disables and boards the sub they find children being smuggled out of the Confederation to escape death squads.

THE FUTURE IS NOW

This episode highlights Nathan Bridger as a man of principle. He refuses to return the refugees, challenging his superior at the UEO. He insists that by doing nothing, the United Earth / Oceans Organization tacitly supports murder.

When the dictator's second in command assassinates his ruler to provide the UEO with a scapegoat, Bridger still refuses to repatriate the refugees. The episode shows more than mindless action adventure.

At first SEAQUEST seemed very much like the old Irwin Allen series VOYAGE TO THE BOTTOM OF THE SEA. As the first season progressed, the series grew better.

In one episode the Seaquest meets an ancient alien spacecraft without degenerating into predictable conflict. The aliens appear to disintegrate people but actually teleport them to a holding cell.

Bridger ultimately swears his crew to secrecy instead of sharing the information with the UEO. He fears the reaction of member nations such as the Amazonian Confederacy.

The Seaquest leads mankind into the future. The UEO, especially Nathan Bridger, wants humanity to become the Earth's cultivator, not her despoiler, and to take humankind beyond previous limits.

SCHEIDER TALKS ABOUT SEAQUEST

Roy Scheider describes the elaborate sets he works on, saying, "The attention to detail in the series is amazing. We have futuristic navigation screens and consoles, even real pools aboard ship with a dolphin."

Scheider admits the series is very ambitious. He says, "It has very high pretensions. Why not? Why not go for what's difficult? The ocean is a wonderful and exciting place, and very nurturing to the planet. This show is about this planet, about the environment and how we're going to have to live in it. The ocean is our background, the submarine is our prop, and we have a cast that I'm enjoying working with very much."

The actor reveals he has always loved the sea. "I like it a lot," he says. "I really do. As a matter of fact I'm building a home on Long Island right now on the ocean. I've been drawn to the sea all my life, just like everyone else has. Since my acquaintanceship with Dr. Ballard, my head is filled with all the wonder and all the things that we don't know about the ocean."

BALLARD AND BRIDGER

Robert Ballard's life provided inspiration for the fictional Nathan Bridger. Ballard worked with Army Intelligence in the 1960s and later commanded attack submarines for the U.S. Navy. He then became a world renowned oceanographer with a doctorate in marine geology and geophysics.

The explorer wrote books, visited the depths of the ocean, and led expeditions making extensive use of camera-equipped, deep-sea diving submersibles. While the discovery of the sunken Titanic is his most publicized accomplishment, he has also found the German battleship Bismark, the greatest warship of World War II.

Ballard dived for the lost fleet off Guadacanal for National Geographic TV. He also probed the mystery of the sinking of the British luxury liner the Lusitania.

Ballard believes in the future of undersea colonies. He says, "There are more people alive today than ever died. In the next 25 years we will have quadrupled the world's population."

Now Ballard serves as senior scientist for the department of applied ocean physics and engineering at Woods Hole Oceanographic Institution in Massachusetts. He also works as the scientific consultant on SEAQUEST DSV.

UNDERSEA LIFE

Ballard believes his seagoing adventures have been as exciting as the fiction of SEAQUEST. He says, "I've seen creatures that are hard to believe; tube worms that are eight feel tall, and underwater pagoda structures. It's just amazing. The average depth of the ocean is 12,000 feet and when you make a dive to that depth you fall like a rock for two-and-a-half hours before you finally arrive. You go through this metamorphosis from a world of sunlight to a two dimensional world and then to a world of darkness and three dimensionality. We fly under the ocean; we don't walk around. You become an underwater bird, so to speak. It's quite a transformation."

The sea life portrayed by special effects on the TV series fascinates Dr. Ballard. "The care that's gone into every detail," he says. "How does a bubble expand on its way up, what's bio-luminescence all about, how do currents work, and how does marine snow interact with the propeller of a submarine as it goes by? To watch that become a real image to where you swear it's reality — it's magic."

OF COURSE IT'S SCIENCE FICTION

Ballard explains, "I think of the series as science fiction, a mix of fiction and fact, and that's what's exciting about it. Because when you watch it, it's very believable. We're still in the Lewis and Clark phase of underwater exploration, that's why SEAQUEST is so credible. It is exactly what we're going to be doing in twenty-five years. It's not science fiction, it's predicting the future."

People involved with science fiction projects don't like to call them science fiction, even if they are. Science fiction projects current realities into the future, providing cautionary tales.

Some episodes of SEAQUEST do this. In one an ecologist buys an old submarine to sink whaling vessels. International law outlawed whaling by 2018.

That episode has a counterpart in the 1990s. The Sea Shepherd Conservation Society, founded in 1977 by former Greenpeace member Paul Watson, uses ships, including a submarine, to disrupt illegal whaling. They place themselves between the whaling ships and their prey. Their existence inspired the SEAQUEST episode about a more radical, futuristic group.

FACING THE FUTURE

Current concerns project into the future in "if this goes on" type storylines. The episode about the Amazonian Confederation and their death squads parallels what is happening today in such nations as Brazil and Guatemala.

Ballard says the series deals with the future as it might very well be. He explains, "Neil Armstrong walked on the moon before we went to the biggest mountain ranges beneath the sea. I really think that the next generation is the generation that will truly explore our planet. In fact, the children watching SEAQUEST are the future explorers. We can turn them on to exploration by showing them the tip of

NATHAN BRIDGER

The pilot reveals much about Captain Nathan Bridger. Subsequent episodes fill in the blanks.

In 2007 Nathan Bridger helped design Project seaQuest, developing the ultimate warrior class submarine. It would be the largest, sleekest, fastest, most deadly vessel ever. The thrill of discovery kept Nathan from remembering he was designing a superior weapon of war.

Then his son, a first year seaman serving on an explorer ship in the Arctic, was killed during a territorial dispute. Suddenly his accomplishments tasted as ashes in his mouth. He realized he was creating a more effective to kill people.

the iceberg, so to speak, with our expeditions. I think we will turn on a generation to explore Earth, and to hopefully save mankind in the nick of time. We're the first generation that's been capable of destroying Earth. I sure hope the next one pulls it out of the fire."

People now working in the space program credit STAR TREK with inspiring them into a career in space exploration. SEAQUEST may excite people about the possibilities beneath the seas.

TOY QUEST

Popular films and television series generate merchandising. Recently science fiction shows have spawned many toy tie-ins. SEAQUEST DSV continues the tradition.

The series of action figures from Playmates toys have fourteen-point articulation. They are much more elaborate than most toys. The figures feature extra mobility to fit into the SEAQUEST vehicles

that began to appear in the spring of 1994.

The action figures include Nathan Bridger, Tim O'Neil, Lucas Wolenczak, Darwin, Manilow Crocker, Jonathan Ford, Katherine Hitchcock, The Regulator, and Dr. Z. Most of the figures fit into an available One-man Attack Sub.

The 25 inch replica of the Seaquest features electronics providing light and sound, articulated rear fins, a spring-launched deep sea probe, and a display stand. Other SEAQUEST toys include a 15 inch "Renegade Delta 4 Submarine" with electronics providing a light-up nuclear reactor propulsion system. A Mini-pickup amphibian craft holds several action figures and offers an operating crane. The toys not released by the summer of 1994 were expected by Christmas 1994.

Science fiction toys often become valuable collectibles. SEAQUEST toys benefit from being more elaborate than most; the Seaquest submarine is an exciting design.

STORMY WATERS

Steven Spielberg's first TV outing, AMAZING STORIES, met with critical drubbing upon its premiere. SEAQUEST fared no better.

The premiere, directed by Irvin Kershner, suffers from a weak story. It looks like a special effects showcase. Howlers such as Shelly Hack's solemn proclamation to Nathan Bridger that, "Captain, you are as impotent as your boat," result in laughter in the wrong places.

Irvin Kershner hasn't directed a good film since his spectacular THE EMPIRE STRIKES BACK in 1980. The astonishingly misguided ROBOCOP II in 1991 completely ignored the first ROBOCOP. His SEAQUEST premiere utterly failed. The series struggles to overcome the bad first impression.

The high ratings of the premiere dropped immediately. Audiences sat through the two hour show, shrugged their shoulders, changed the channel, and never changed back. The show went into a ratings slide and hit 83rd place out of 132 prime-time network series. The position would be a death knell for almost any show except SEAQUEST DSV. It was renewed for a second season.

The series struggled to reinvent itself in its first season. A lot of rethinking took place. Early in the series, Phil Segal, an executive for Amblin Entertainment, described SEAQUEST to Bill Warren of STARLOG by saying, "When you look at the society today, and project it into the future, things won't change when we populate the ocean. Man won't grow gills and walk into the sea."

About a year after Segal made that statement, a scientist, played by Charlton Heston, developed gills to breathe underwater in the series. It is safe to label that science fiction.

TOUGH VOYAGING

The show underwent an important transformation. Bland confrontations of early episodes were

Nathan resigned his Naval commission. He and his wife moved to a remote tropical island to cut themselves off from civilization.

In 2015 his wife became critically ill from a tropical respiratory disease. Time was lost before medical assistance could arrive on the remote island. by then it was too late. His wife died before his eyes.

Alone, Nathan threw himself into pure research, including his dolphin intelligence experiments involving Darwin. Then one morning in 2018 a Navy helicopter landed on his island.

His old friend Admiral Noyce stepped out. Noyce told Nathan the Seaquest was going to be turned over to the recently formed United Earth/Oceans

Organization. They wanted Nathan to assume command on the research vessel. Nathan refused, but agree to visit his dream made real.

Shortly after arriving, Nathan discovered that the Seaquest was underway. Noyce assured him he could leave at any time, but the vessel must investigate a report of a rogue sub menacing undersea colonies.

Nathan felt manipulated when he discovered Darwin aboard. He finally decided to stay rather than remain alone on his island.

replaced by stories that said something.

An unusual episode features William Shatner as a dictator on the run. He allows himself to be captured to help a young son traumatized by witnessing his mother's death at the hands of his father's enemies. Shatner delivered a carefully understated performance, his best acting since STAR TREK II—THE WRATH OF KHAN.

May 22nd saw the season finale of SEAQUEST DSV. It ended with Nathan Bridger destroying the Seaquest to seal a rupture in the crust of the ocean floor.

The submarine of the title is gone. Where does this leave the series?

The episode ends with Nathan Bridger telling Lucas it's time for a new Seaquest. In reality it takes years to build a vessel of the size and capability of Seaquest. That's TV for you; blow it up this month, rebuild it the next.

The last few episodes of SEAQUEST emphasize science fiction. Executive producers Patrick Hasburgh and David Burke's 20 page

outline for the second season places strong emphasis on science fiction and fantasy. They want to convince audiences SEAQUEST is now very different than they remember.

NBC renewed the series that finished fourth in its time period for the season, falling behind CBS' MURDER SHE WROTE, ABC's LOIS & CLARK: THE NEW ADVENTURES OF SUPERMAN, and the Fox Network comedies MARTIN and LIVING SINGLE. The demographics saved the show. Its viewers consist of the coveted 18-49 age group.

SPIELBERG SPEAKS OUT

Steven Spielberg's Amblin Entertainment endured much flack because of their television productions. First AMAZING STORIES lasted two years only because the network made a two year commitment in advance. It failed with critics and audiences.

Their prime time animated series FAMILY DOG disappeared from the network schedule before it premiered in 1991. It returned for retooling until the summer of 1993. Then CBS dumped it into the summer schedule with little fanfare. It garnered worse reviews than AMAZING STORIES and died a quick death.

Critics were ready to hate SEAQUEST. The show began with serious story problems. Spielberg admitted in an interview with Tom Shales published in December 1993, "The show has disappointed me. The potential of the show and some of the scripts I'm now reading are wonderful. We just hope the audience will continue to give it a chance, because some of the scripts coming up are terrific."

Spielberg revealed that he was forced to distance himself from the show while he made SCHINDLER'S LIST. He said, "I had a lot to do with SEAQUEST before I went to Poland. Once I went to Poland, I was out of touch for a long, long time, so I didn't have a lot to do with the series, because I was in

another world, literally, in another time. Under water was the least of my concerns.

"What I should have done," he continued, "which I wish I had done, was delay SEAQUEST for a year. SEAQUEST should have come out in the fall of '94 as opposed to the fall of '93, because then I would have been around every day, and I think it would have been a little bit different."

YEAR TWO— A NEW BEGINNING

NBC Entertainment President Warren Littlefield talked about the future of SEAQUEST in the April 30, 1994 LOS ANGELES TIMES. He said, "We're simply looking at the problems, the quality of work and where we think the series can go. We also believe there is a creative vision at Amblin and with the executive producers, and we believe, given the time and preparation, they can execute that vision."

David J. Burke, the executive producer hired to put the show on course early in the first season, explained the problems, saying, "I had a problem last season because this show leaned on Ballard before it leaned on guys who do what I do. This is still television. Some of the production problems resulted from trying to deal with a show born out of science first and television second."

The bridge of the submarine seats crew members facing the monitors on the wall with their backs to Captain Bridger. The redesigned submarine will change this so that the crew face the captain.

New crew will join Scheider aboard the seaQuest. New cast members include Edward Kerr as Lt. James Brody, a cocky special weapons and tactics expert; Rosalind Allen as Dr. Wendy Smith, a biophysicist and psychologist gifted with ESP; Michael DeLuise as Tony Piccolo, a misfit who was physically altered as a result of a scientific experiment; Peter DeLuise as Dagwood, the ship's janitor, who comes from a genetically engineered race known as "Daggers"; and Kathy Evison as Ensign Henderson, a naive newcomer.

Burke says the new science fiction "is a lot more fun to write because it's finally about human conflict, not fighting battles over who owns mineral rights."

He believes the series will enjoy a healthy future after retooling. "This was a very good idea," he insists, "that got off on very poor footing, but it remained a very good idea. It was a behemoth of a show technically, and it took all year to get that managed. In some ways, running a leaner operation will make this a better show. When you're up against the wall and running hard to stay on schedule, there's this throw-money-at-it attitude. I think it's better to throw your creativity at it, which is what we're doing now."

The fall of 1994 will see a different SEAQUEST DSV surface on NBC.

Superman has been a popular staple on television since the early '50s. The '90s TV version focuses more on characterization than costumed antics. Time will tell if this proves as enduring.

LOIS & CLARK

Superman on TV is not a new idea. The early 1950s witnessed the first TV version of the Man of Steel. This lasted several years. Middle-aged television viewers remember THE ADVENTURES OF SUPERMAN starring George Reeves as a beloved part of their childhood.

Superman continued on TV in animated cartoons. In 1978 the first of four movies starring Christopher Reeve appeared. The studios released the last Superman movie in 1987.

When discussions arose about creating a new Superman TV series, they decided to retool it for the '90s. While the 1950s series offered strictly action and adventure, the motion pictures introduced a strong romantic element between Superman and Lois Lane.

Romance between Superman and Lois ran hot and cool in the comic books over the years. It often seemed a very one-sided affair as Lois pined for a Man of Steel who kept his distance.

Dean Cain and Teri Hatcher of LOIS & CLARK: THE NEW ADVENTURES OF SUPERMAN.

Photo ©1994 Al Ortega

Recent comics changed this. Clark asked Lois to marry him and revealed his secret identity to her. The movies and comics made it inevitable the TV series would place love first.

The new Superman television show appeals to all age groups. Described as "MOONLIGHTING meets SUPERMAN," the show placed emphasis on characterization from the premiere.

The complete title of the series is LOIS & CLARK: THE NEW ADVENTURES OF SUPERMAN. David Jacobs acts as executive producer and Deborah Joy LeVine as co-executive producer and developer for the Roundelay Production in association with Warner Brothers Television series. Bryce Zabel serves as supervising producer, Dusty Kay as co-supervising producer, Thania St. John and Mel Efros as producers and Robert Butler as executive consultant.

ONE MINUTE IN THE FUTURE

Press releases describe the show as "set just one minute into the future." Action takes place in the fictional city of Metropolis and Clark's boyhood home town of Smallville. It all films on the Warner Brothers backlot.

A twenty-eight year old Clark looks for his place in the world. Deborah Joy LeVine wrote the premiere episode. She has also written some of the best episodes of the first season.

Her two hour series premiere established the mix of humor, characterization, and adventure that defines the series. Some Superman fans want a grimmer, more hard driving series, but the average television viewer lured in by the premiere liked what they saw.

Head-to-head competition between SEAQUEST and Superman continued throughout the year. LOIS & CLARK failed to top the ratings but it finished 20 ratings points better than SEAQUEST.

Neither show wants to wear the science fiction emblem. Both appeal to audiences who like fantastic adventures. They were the only two shows in that category on the three major networks. Programming them opposite each other diluted their audience.

LOIS & CLARK ran the pilot episode a second time as a two-parter on weeknights. They tried to lure a wider audience to its regular time slot on Sunday nights.

SEAQUEST suffered when pitted against LOIS & CLARK, yet NBC announced it will return to the same time slot. The fall of 1994 will pit new episodes of LOIS & CLARK against new episodes of SEAQUEST DSV. It seems the series believe switching time slot would be an admission of defeat.

A NEW STYLE OF SUPERMAN

LOIS & CLARK offers a very modern sensibility. The 1978 SUPERMAN:

THE NEW SCI FI TV BOOK

SIDEBAR

A MODERN LOIS LANE

Teri Hatcher plays Lois Lane. She was born in Sunnyvale, California and studied acting at the American Conservatory Theatre. She made her motion picture debut in THE BIG PICTURE then had a large role playing Sylvester Stallone's sister in TANGO AND CASH. She co-starred or played supporting roles in the comedies SOAPDISH and STRAIGHT TALK.

Teri starred in the short-lived Norman Lear sitcom SUNDAY DINNER and appeared on episodes of L.A. LAW, SEINFELD, MacGYVER, and MURPHY BROWN. Her Lois Lane appears stern, self-possessed, and capable of wry humor. Career woman Lois Lane considers friend-

THE MOVIE introduces Clark Kent when he moves to Metropolis. The TV series follows suit.

LeVine brings feeling and delicate sensibility to the series. Audiences like these characters.

Zabel, the supervising producer, says, "Deborah's the person who wrote the pilot. She's been involved since the beginning. I think there are a lot of people at the network who feel a great deal of comfort knowing she's around here. Deborah has a very distinctive voice. I think she's done some absolutely great things. I think it would be a loss to lose her."

He continues, "Having said all that, I think the real star of the show is Superman. I think there is a dynamic that is so great it's almost Shakespearean. I also think the show dynamic of the triangle is something you can't beat. You have Lois, Clark, and Superman. Lois loves Superman. Clark loves Lois. Lois doesn't love Clark. Clark, by being Superman, has created his own blocking character. It doesn't get any better than that. To me, that dynamic is the star of the

show that could keep it going for a good, long time."

Dean Cain plays Superman and Clark Kent. Cain hails from Mt. Clemens, Michigan. He graduated from Princeton University after becoming an All-American football star.

His performance on the gridiron captured the NCAA record for the most interceptions in one season. It landed him a spot with the Buffalo Bills. Sidelined with a knee injury, he pursued acting.

Dean's father, Christopher Cain, directed the 1984 film THE STONE BOY. Dean played a supporting role.

More recently Dean appeared as Rick on BEVERLY HILLS 90210 and made guest appearances on LIFE GOES ON, A DIFFERENT WORLD, and GRAPEVINE. Dean also writes, but none of his screenplays were filmed. He developed a project called NAKED TV.

THE ADVENTURES OF LOIS & CLARK

Previous filmed versions of Superman concentrated on stories centering entirely on the Man of Steel. Supporting characters, including Clark Kent, occupied very secondary roles. LOIS & CLARK: THE NEW ADVENTURES OF SUPERMAN reverses that.

Bryce Zabel told COMICS INTERVIEW, "Clearly, LOIS & CLARK is not a Superman series, it's a Lois and Clark series. Clark happens to be Superman so there's that large element of it. Essentially, the relationship is the driving force here.

"As with any story about a relationship," he continued, "there are certain marks you're going to hit. There are certain places where you can't go back, you can only go forward. A lot of times in the relationship, the people who were involved in it are saying, 'What are we doing here? Let's get married or let's call it quits.' I'd assume Lois and Clark could eventually come to that place. If they do get married, isn't the logical thing for them to try to have children? If they do, what kind of children are they? I think it could be fascinating new

ground. I, for one, am very positively hopeful that the series will stay around. If I'm on it or not, I want to watch it."

This series Clark Kent adopted his costumed persona as an adult, the approach taken in the '50s TV series and recent motion pictures. Kent wants to establish his civilian persona and resorts to Superman only in extreme danger.

The first season finale emphasizes that Clark Kent needs to know that Lois Lane loves him for himself before he'll reveal his dual identity. Otherwise he'll always fear she loves him for being Superman, not who he is inside.

THE UFO CONNECTION

LOIS & CLARK possessed a clear sense of self right out of the gate. In the second episode, "Strange Visitor (From Another Planet)," Clark finds the spaceship that brought him to Earth in a secret government warehouse.

ships of utmost importance. She reveals emotions, giving the character many facets.

A costumed hero without mask that isn't recognized in his civilian identity posed an early problem for the producers. "In the beginning of this season a lot of us had a lot of problems with it," Zabel explains. "It is, essentially, ridiculous. Superman looks like Clark. Clark looks like Superman. A pair of glasses isn't going to disguise anybody. We don't even have the hat that George Reeves got to wear. So there is a great deal of similarity. There's no getting around that. It is a problem. My response is, the fact that Lois doesn't recognize Clark to be Superman is the 'magic if' of the series. It's been the 'magic if' for nearly 60 years of Superman. If you don't buy it, you're not going to enjoy the show.

"There's nothing anybody from a writing or directorial point of view is ever going to be able to do to change that particular reference point about Clark and Superman. The thing you do is not call attention to it," he concludes.

Bryce Zabel wrote the episode. He says, "It was literally about Clark finding out that he came in a spaceship, finding the spaceship, and realizing—and I thought this was an interesting twist for him—that he wasn't Russian. What would you conclude if you were Jonathan and Martha Kent? You found a spaceship with a little baby in it in 1966. You wouldn't say, 'Look at this alien.' It's a little baby. It's a kid. You'd think, 'Did those crazy Russians put something up there? Did our people do this?' It was a nice co-mingling of mythos there. There's a whole UFO mythology and a whole Superman mythology. If you think about it, they dovetail perfectly. Superman becomes one of the original Operation Blue Book UFO sightings in the '60s. It fits perfectly with Dean Cain's age, which I believe is 28."

Terence Knox guest starred as Jason Trask, a government agent who thinks Superman is not of this Earth. Driven by this knowledge, he believes Superman a threat to humanity due to the superpowers. Trask wants to destroy Superman for the good of all.

Trask is willing to do anything or kill anyone to achieve his ends. When Lois and Clark are prisoners on an airplane, Trask pushes them out to attract Superman's attention. The scene projects great drama, and effective characterization.

Trask lures Superman to his destruction by threatening the lives of innocent people because he thinks Superman is a menace! This storyline remains unresolved. A few weeks later, one of the best episodes of the series, followed.

In the next episode, "Neverending Battle," Luthor returns in a story that brings Superman and Luthor into direct contact. Superman intrigues Luthor. He decides to test the limits of the Man of Steel by placing people in danger and creating disasters.

When Superman realizes innocent people are endangered because of him, he considers quitting, something Lex Luthor wants. Ultimately, resisting Luthor prevents Clark from hanging up his cape forever.

SUPER MANIA

"I'm Looking Through You" deals realistically with the Superman mania sweeping through Metropolis. People start merchandising the likeness of the Man of Steel.

The exploitation for profit bothers Superman. He makes sure the proceeds are distributed to the needy rather than the greedy. A subplot involves an invisible man.

"Requiem for a Superhero" pits Superman against bionic men nearly as strong as he is. Lois Lane's estranged father invented the bionic men. This troubles Lois, creating the basis for the character angle of the story.

A funny bit shows Clark using his powers to create a phony earthquake. The series films in Burbank. Three months later earthquake jokes lost their humor.

Teri Hatcher and her husband.

Photo ©1994 Al Ortega

SIDEBAR

THE NEW PERRY WHITE

Perry White is essential to any Superman series. The character role didn't figure prominently in the recent movie series. The 1950s TV series elevated the role to a main part. LOIS & CLARK: THE NEW ADVENTURES OF SUPERMAN follows in this TV tradition.

As Perry White, Lane Smith brings the right gruffness and vulnerability to the role. Perry stands out as an individual.

The seasoned veteran on LOIS & CLARK is Lane Smith. He previously appeared in more than 100 feature films, miniseries, and TV shows. His performance as President Richard Nixon in the miniseries THE

Paul Power plays one of the bionic boxers. He also works as the storyboard artist on LOIS & CLARK, designing Superman's flying sequences. Power fought as an amateur boxer in his native Australia.

The TV Superman isn't the unstoppable powerhouse of the comic books. This Superman can be placed in jeopardy.

"I've Got A Crush On You" fits the MOONLIGHTING vein. Lois Lane and Clark Kent go undercover at a nightclub. Superman appears less than in any other episode in the series.

"The Green, Green Glow of Home" continues from the earlier "Strange Visitor (From Another Planet)." Trask wants to finish what he started.

He finds kryptonite, its first appearance in the series. Smallville appeared in previous episodes. When Trask finds kryptonite near the Kent's place, he quarantines the area.

This attracts Clark's attention. Lois thinks it's a government cover up, but doesn't suspect Trask.

THE ADVENTURES OF CLARK KENT

Trask threatens to kill the Kents because they betrayed humanity by helping the alien enemy. He believes Superman prepares the way for an invasion from space. Trask wants to kill this alien emissary.

Kryptonite robs Superman of his powers. After escaping its influence, it takes time to regain strength.

With only normal human strength, Clark attacks Trask. They wage a knock-down, drag-out fight ending when the Smallville sheriff kills Trask. The sheriff involves himself after watching Trask pull a gun to shoot Clark in the back.

The viewer expects Trask to die after he learns Superman's secret identity. A bullet solved the problem.

LOIS & CLARK normally shows little violence. "The Green, Green Glow of Home" displays more violence than three average episodes combined. The story dictates the need for violence. It is not gratuitous.

Trask earns his violent death. In one scene he plots to set a house afire with the Kents tied up inside.

Bryce Zabel describes "Strange Visitor" and its sequel, "The Green, Green Glow of Home," by saying, "In the first episode ('Strange Visitor'), the jeopardy was that Lois could be hurt or that his identity would be lost. That gives us a real jeopardy. Those have nothing to do with Doomsday stalking in. It's a lot easier to do Doomsday in a comic book than on TV. In 'The Green, Green Glow of Home,' the real jeopardy is that Clark becomes a normal guy because of the kryptonite and that this Trask madman can kick his ass. Clark has to protect himself and his family that he loves strictly through the force of his goodness."

A CLASSIC HOMAGE

Romantic episodes dominated the first season. "Pheromone, My Lovely" typifies this story type. It told a story about a perfume which induced interest in a member of the opposite sex.

The romances appeared too different from the adventure stories to appeal to the same audience. Emphasis switches to adventure stories in the second season. The change began in the second half of the first season. Action in the episodes increased dramatically.

Additional footage appeared in the two hour pilot when it ran again on December 22 and December 29, 1993. The two hour story originally filled a one hour and forty-five minute slot.

"All Shook Up" pays homage to the 1950s episode of THE ADVENTURES OF SUPERMAN titled "Panic In The Sky." Dialogue in the episodes sounds different, but the basic plot is the same. Superman flies into space to stop an asteroid threatening the Earth. The collision gives Superman amnesia.

"Illusions of Grandeur" offers an amusing story in

FINAL DAYS, attracted favorable critical notice. He also played major roles for other miniseries, including SPECIAL BULLETIN, DRESS GRAY, and A RUMOR OF WAR. He portrayed a continuing part in the TV series "V." Smith's films include roles in THE MIGHTY DUCKS, MY COUSIN VINNIE, RED DAWN, PRINCE OF THE CITY, NETWORK, and PLACES IN THE HEART.

On Broadway he appeared in the Pulitzer Prize-winning play "Glengarry Glen Ross" for which he won a Drama Desk Award. Other stage work includes "Modigliani," "Berchtesgaden," "Visions of Kerouca," "The Love Death Plays," and more than 600 performances as McMurphy in "One Flew Over the Cuckoo's Nest" on the New York stage.

THE NEW JIMMY OLSEN

Young Michael Landes got his start with a recurring role on the first couple years of THE WONDER YEARS. He plays Jimmy Olsen, "cub reporter." Unlike past TV and film characterizations, this version of Jimmy enjoys an interesting friendship with Perry White, who clearly considers himself Jimmy's mentor.

This Jimmy Olsen differs greatly from the '50s Olsen played by Jack Larsen. Phyllis Coates, the original series Lois Lane, says the modern Jimmy is, "a really sensitive, thoughtful, perceptive young man and quite different from 'golly, gee whiz, jeepers,'" of the Jack Larson version. "That used to drive us

which Penn Jillette, of Penn & Teller, appears as an obnoxious magician suspected of committing murder and kidnapping rich children for ransom.

In "Foundling," Clark investigates his past. David Warner appears as Jor-El, Superman's Kryptonian father, in a flashback.

THE OTHER SUPERMAN

Luthor learns how to create a clone of Superman in "Vatman." He intends to destroy the Man of Steel.

The story works better than your usual "evil twin" gimmick. The twin believes Superman is evil and must be destroyed. Superman talks his twin into seeing the light.

Bryce Zabel explains the reasoning behind the episode, saying, "You have a hero who's as powerful as Superman, who are you going to put him up against? If you follow this rule, nothing can cross this line; it gets harder and harder to find real jeopardy for him. As a consequence you have to look for something that can match it.

What can match him but a clone of him? A lot of shows that are struggling in their 12th season, they'll have the evil twin of Linda Gray come out. Well, for us to go to the evil twin in the first season was a bit premature, except that it was Superman, and where else are you going to get it?"

"Fly Hard" uses little of Superman. Instead it creates an interesting situation when criminals invade the Daily Planet building and take everyone hostage.

Clark must not expose his dual identity. Lex Luthor is also a hostage and has nothing to do with the crime.

Clark tries to remain passive, but must act heroic to save the lives of his friends. He proves Superman isn't the only hero in Metropolis.

Jack, played by Chris Demetral, returns in this episode. An unspoken understanding develops between Jack and Clark.

At first Clark disappoints Jack when he won't stand up to the gunmen. Later, when Clark leaps down a flight of stairs to tackle a man shooting at them, Jack realizes there is more to Clark than meets the eye. Although he never says so, events reveal to Jack that Clark is Superman. He never confronts Clark with his suspicions.

LEX AND LOIS

The season finale held many surprises. The two part story, "Barbarians at The Planet" and "The House of Luthor," covers much ground.

Lex Luthor snows Lois Lane. She buys his veneer of respectability. He gradually woos her all season.

In "Barbarians at The Planet," Lex asks Lois to marry him. She says she has to think about it because of her friends at the Daily Planet.

No one says no to Lex Luthor. He secretly destabilizes the newspaper by forcing its advertisers to withdraw. Lex then magnanimously buys the newspaper keeping anyone from being fired.

He then engineers the bombing of the Daily Planet building. This puts the paper out of business. Luthor frames Jack for the crime.

Lois agrees to marry Lex and takes a job at his cable news network (LNN). Clark cannot convince Lois that Lex is evil without revealing his secret identity. He never goes to her as Superman to tell what he knows.

Superman goes to Lois to learn if she loves him for himself. He decides Lois only loves Superman, not Clark, and leaves her with her decision to marry Luthor. She admits she'd turn Lex down for Superman.

THE RETURN OF PHYLLIS COATES

The big wedding scene in "The House of Luthor" provides the perfect opportunity for a homage to the 1950s Superman series. Phyllis Coates plays Lois Lane's mother. During the first season of THE ADVENTURES OF SUPERMAN, more than 40 years ago, Phyllis Coates played Lois Lane opposite George Reeves' Superman.

up the wall," Coates admits.

Landes appeared on THIRTYSOME-THING as the teenage version of the Ken Olin character. He played recurring parts on such series as THE TORKELSONS and THE FRESH PRINCE OF BEL AIR. He also appeared in the afternoon specials, RETURN TO HIP HOP HIGH and PLEASE GOD, I'M ONLY 17. He co-starred in the low budget feature films AN AMERICAN SUMMER and WHEN THE PARTY'S OVER.

SIDEBAR

A LEX LUTHOR FOR THE NINETIES

Lex Luthor appeared in almost every first season episode. North Conway, New Hampshire born John Shea portrays the character. The actor grew up in Springfield, Massachusetts and acquired his undergraduate degree at Bates College.

He discovered his talent for acting in college. Shea went on to earn a master's degree in directing from the Yale School of Drama.

His first professional acting job was on Broadway in the lead of "Yentl." The part earned him the Theatre World Award as Most Promising Newcomer. Many other stage roles followed, including

Noel Neil played Lois Lane for laughs. Coates portrayed an abrasive, tough-as-nails journalist. She took whatever the bad guys threw at her. Her Lois appeared as no-nonsense as that of Teri Hatcher. Teri's Lois shows more heart and soul, though.

Coates' Lois tested the lame excuses Clark Kent gave for his disappearances when Superman appeared. The woman never got the chance to be more than a hard-nosed journalist. Fictional females on TV in the '50s appeared either hard or soft. The episodes with Phyllis Coates remain some of the best of that classic series.

"My son said this is a gestalt, and it is—it's kind of something going full circle," Coates says in an interview with THE LOS ANGELES TIMES. Describing her early days in television's infancy, the actress reveals, "I had no wardrobe mistress and no hairdresser in those days. Oh boy—I had one suit! One suit, and a double in case I got egg on it! George's dresser dressed me. My makeup man was

Harry Thomas, who made up every monster in Hollywood."

Teri Hatcher first wanted Phyllis Coates to play her mother. A mutual friend mentioned that Teri and Phyllis should get together for lunch.

When they wrote the wedding script, Teri suggested Lois Lane's mother should attend, and who better to play the part? Teri suggested it to executive producer Deborah Joy Levine. Levine immediately rewrote the script to include Lois' mother in the cast of characters.

HER TURN

Noel Neill played Lois Lane in the movie serials and on 76 of the 1950s TV episodes. Many still identify her with Lois Lane. She played Lois' mother in a brief scene in the 1978 film SUPERMAN: THE MOVIE. So clearly Phyllis Coates turn had come.

"It's true I was never as identified with Lois Lane as other people have been," admits Coates. "I've done other things and I'm not one to live in the past. I was delighted that Teri would think of me. When I came on the set, I said, 'Make me look like her mother, not like her grandmother!'"

Unlike Teri Hatcher, Phyllis Coates could never explore her character or express genuine romantic interest in Superman. She quit the series after only one year. She recalls, "I would have shaped the character a little differently. I would have played her with a little more dimension. In those days I couldn't even smile at Superman. If I even gave a knowing or suggestive look to him. . . I was like a horse with a bit in his mouth! I played her tough and direct. I had one or two attitudes and that was it."

Coates praises the character as played by Teri Hatcher. She says, "Lois is a woman of the '90s—she's sexy and she gets to play comedy—and I got to do none of that. It's great to see her fulfilling the role. She's the best Lois Lane, really, ever."

One of the nicest dramatic character turns in the series occurs in

"Barbarians At The Planet" when Clark admits his love to Lois. Although she responds that she only likes him as a friend, she later reconsiders as she's preparing to wed Lex.

THE LUTHOR QUESTION

Even as Luthor prepares to marry Lois and reform, he secures a piece of kryptonite and lures Superman into a deathtrap. His plot against the Daily Planet ultimately defeats Luthor.

Perry White, Jimmy Olsen, and Jack investigate. Their evidence proves Lex masterminded the bombing of the planet. The police confront Lex on the chapel steps right after Lois admits she can't go through with it.

Luthor flips. He commits suicide by leaping from his own penthouse balcony. Headlines report that his body disappeared from the morgue. A window of possibility remains open.

Unfortunately Luthor leaped off the tallest building in Metropolis. His body

"American Days," "The Dining Room," "Romeo and Juliet," and "End of the World."

His feature films include the critically acclaimed Costa Gavras' film MISSING, and WINDY CITY, which won him the Montreal Film Festival's Best Actor Award. He also appeared in STEALING HOME, FREEJACK, A NEW LIFE, and HONEY, I BLEW UP THE BABY.

Shea achieved recognition in TV movies and miniseries including SMALL SACRIFICES, HAVE YOU SEEN THE MUFFIN MAN?, and BABY M, for which he won an Emmy Award. He also appeared in THE IMPOSSIBLE SPY, DEADLY FORCE, and the miniseries KENNEDY. He starred opposite Mimi Rogers in LADY KILLER and in a remake of the

Hitchcock classic NOTORIOUS

Shea played a starring role on the short-lived, but critically acclaimed, TV series WIOU. He also appeared in the feature film DEAD WRONG.

Shea lives in New York City with his wife, photographer Laura Pettibone, and son, Jake.

John Shea's Lex Luthor is different from the comic books. He has hair.

should have smashed to a wet spot on the pavement.

Addressing the Luthor question, Bryce Zabel states, "Depending on what the network and studio think about the actor and the part, he might be dead. He might be coming back. That's unclear. In terms of the overall series, whether Lois and Clark are widely apart or sort of together, we resolve that. Lois will not marry Lex Luthor but Lois and Clark will not quite achieve synchronicity."

This opportunity fails to advance the relationship between Lois and Clark. Instead a hurt Clark claims he confessed love only to dissuade her from marrying Luthor. Lois almost admits she loves Clark at this point, but his claim forces her to remain silent. The hurt in her eyes is clearly visible.

Will their relationship grow? Clark must first realize Lois really loves him. Lois never knew Clark loved her until he said so. Clark never revealed this before because he wants Lois to love him and not only Superman.

A DOWN TO EARTH CLARK KENT

The Clark Kents shown in THE ADVENTURES OF SUPERMAN in the '50s and the Superman movies of the '70s and '80s differ in many ways. Yet both guard their thoughts and feelings.

The new Clark Kent played by Dean Cain displays his feelings. He says what he thinks.

"Barbarians At The Planet" offers a scene when Clark honestly and articulately blurts out how he feels. This presents him as a human being, grounding the character in reality even if he does wear a costume under his street clothes and can fly to outer space in the wink of an eye.

In another scene Superman observes Lois accepting the engagement ring from Lex Luthor, then flies to the North Pole. Amid the icy wastes, he screams his rage and grief into the desolate sky. The woman he loves plans to marry the most evil man he knows, and not all his powers can prevent it.

LOIS & CLARK: THE NEW ADVENTURES OF

SUPERMAN centers on a love triangle. Although Lois is initially enamored of Superman while barely aware of Clark, Clark and Lois grow closer during the season. Lois realizes cares about Clark. She shares many experiences with Clark.

WRITING FOR LOIS & CLARK

Production of an episode of LOIS & CLARK takes anywhere from four days to four weeks to write. Time allowed for writing varies based on the time of the season. Production moves at a relaxed pace during the beginning of the season. Later deadlines tighten.

The director expects to have the script in hand eight days before shooting. He then "preps" it getting the storyboards ready, particularly for special effects. He knows he has what he needs to go before the camera. Shooting of each one-hour episode takes eight days, including special effects.

Teri Hatcher and Dean Cain of LOIS & CLARK: THE NEW ADVENTURES OF SUPERMAN.

Photo ©1994 Al Ortega

LOIS & CLARK: THE NEW ADVENTURES OF SUPERMAN brings audiences more intimate stories than the theatrical version. The four modern Superman feature films offer bits and pieces. The new TV series stretches those moments.

The 22 hours of the first season builds the personas of every character, including Jimmy Olsen and Perry White. They emerge from the background in a grander adventure. Lex Luthor plays to better effect than in any movie.

The new Lex Luthor must captivate for many episodes. He skates the edge but stays just out of reach of the law. Superman knows Luthor perpetrates many nefarious schemes but lacks the evidence to bring Luthor to justice. Ultimately, like the greatest criminals in history, Luthor believes himself invincible and gets sloppy. That brings his ultimate downfall.

THE STYLE OF STORYTELLING

The 1950s THE ADVENTURES OF SUPERMAN is an entertaining artifact of another era. Characterizations and storytelling appear simple.

The '90s version creates a believable world for an unbelievable character—a man in a red and blue suit who flies. This version of Superman presents the character as a believable human being for the first time. The films made Superman real but Clark Kent merely a place to hide. Those films only live when Clark becomes Superman.

LOIS & CLARK: THE NEW ADVENTURES OF SUPERMAN gives both Superman and Clark Kent individual personas. Clark becomes as interesting as Superman. The show reverses the movies. Clark Kent is real and Superman merely the persona he adopts to use his powers.

Most superhero productions make audiences wait for the costumed hero to emerge before becoming interesting. The best do not. Their stories involve the viewer in the lives of ordinary people. This is the real strength of THE NEW ADVENTURES OF SUPERMAN.

THE EPISODE THAT NEVER WAS

The producers discussed a twist on Superman's origin. Black and white flashbacks could tell the story of Jor-el (Superman's father) visiting Earth in 1946. Jor-el would meet a man in Kansas. When Krypton faced destruction, Jor-el would send his son to the place in Kansas where this man lived 20 years before. In the elapsed time, the Kents had bought the property.

Because Warner Brothers series HOMEFRONT ended shortly before, the producers of LOIS & CLARK had easy access to 1940s costumes and props. Dean Cain would have played Jor-el.

DC comics' Mike Carlin opposed the idea. Warner listened to him. Bryce Zabel believes D.C. should publish the idea as an Elseworlds alternate reality story.

The cast of regulars on BABYLON 5.

The only new non-STAR TREK series currently in first run set in outer space differs from all the non-STAR TREK earthbound series. Only this series goes head-to-head against STAR TREK for the intergalactic TV championship.

By Trey Causey and James Van Hise

BABYLON 5

Early in 1993 series science fiction on television seemed about to experience a renaissance. The pilots of three new series aired at almost the same time.

DEEP SPACE NINE, the second STAR TREK spin-off, debuted in the same month CBS introduced the short-lived SPACE RANGERS. The third series, BABYLON 5, drew attention. For the first time a science fiction series challenged the STAR TREK franchise.

MYSTERIES IN SPACE

In the year 2258 Babylon 5 polices a sector of neutral territory between five hostile confederations, four alien and one human. A representative from each confederation stays on the station serving on an advisory council. The commander of Babylon 5, Jeffrey Sinclair, casts the deciding vote.

The space station fuses a Casablanca style freeport with a mini United Nations. The first three stations were mysteriously destroyed. The fourth disappeared. Babylon 5 is the galaxy's last hope for peace.

The oldest confederation, the Minbari Republic, fought a war against the Earth Alliance. The seemingly victorious Minbari attack force fought their way to Earth then surrendered on the eve of victory.

A circling of starships known as "The Line" protected Earth. No one but a handful of Minbari know why they surrendered. Delenn, their ambassador to Babylon 5, knows the reason.

Jeffrey Sinclair served on the line in the battle. He blacked out while flying a kamikaze mission against one of the Minbari ships. At that time he had sixteen hours of air left in his ship. When he awoke forty-eight hours later, he still had fifteen hours of air left. During the missing time, the Minbari surrendered.

An episode of BABYLON 5 revealed that Sinclair's ship was captured by a Minbari ship. He encountered a group of hooded Minbari in a room. Delenn was among them.

A MINBARI MYSTERY WOMAN

Mira Furlan plays Delenn, one of Babylon 5's many mysteries. Outwardly she appears committed to peace and cooperation between her people and the Earth Alliance. Secretly she wants the reason for the Minbari Surrender to remain hidden.

The deeply religious Minbari may have surrendered because of a prophecy. The head of military operations committed suicide before the war ended. Earth Prime never learned the reason.

Popular actress Mira Furlan left her native Yugoslavia with her husband when civil war broke out. She tried out for the part of Ambassador Delenn when the producers wanted a woman to make the character androgynous. They later abandoned that approach.

It takes three hours every day to put on her makeup for the role. It completely disguises her normal appearance. She still projects so strong a character that all eyes fix on her when Ambassador Delenn enters a room.

The once great empire of the Centauri Republic is in decline. They once ruled hundreds of worlds, but now only a few. Ignoring their fading power, they turn inward growing decadent and hedonistic.

Peter Jurasik plays Lando Mallori, the Centauri ambassador to Babylon 5. The fat, arrogant, womanizing gambler yearns for the Republic's faded glory. He looks for a return power to his people.

The Narn Regime is the youngest of the superpowers. The Centauri Republic once controlled Narn space. The enslaved Narns recently rebelled against their rulers and founded their own empire. They now seek to expand their territory.

Ambassador G'Kar, played by Andreas

The Babylon 5 space station.

Katsulas, represents them on Babylon 5. G'Kar wants Babylon 5 to fail. Then his people could take advantage of the ensuing chaos. The consummate schemer, G'Kar covertly works to this end, keeping in the shadows.

Andreas Katsulas also played an alien for STAR TREK—THE NEXT GENERATION. He portrayed Romulan Commander Tomalak, seen in "The Enemy," "The Defector," and "Future Imperfect." He also played a newcomer named Coolok on the TV series ALIEN NATION.

His other TV work includes appearances on MAX HEADROOM and the tele-movie THE DEATH OF THE INCREDIBLE HULK. Prior to working on television he appeared in the motion pictures SOMEONE TO WATCH OVER ME, THE SICILIAN, and SUNSET.

The actor suggested Ambassador G'Kar not have humanoid hands. Since his head looked so unusual, he reasoned such a being would not have ordinary hands. He reject-ed gloves, believing they look fake. Casts of alien hands were made for him.

AN OASIS IN SPACE

The enigmatic Vorlon Empire recently opened relations with Earth. No human, before the BABYLON 5 pilot, ever saw a Vorlon without their arcane "encounter suits." They wear the suits outside their natural environment.

The mysterious Kosh Naranek represents the Vorlon. No one can predict his rare council votes.

The last of the superpowers, the Earth Alliance, owns and maintains Babylon 5. Martian born Commander Jeffrey Sinclair runs operations and acts as Earth ambassador to the Babylon 5 council. The Minbari accept no one else.

Babylon 5 measures two and a half kilometers in length. It contains many different atmospheres and gravities. Modular sections rotate at different speeds to create the gravities.

Most stories occur aboard Babylon 5. They

involve conflict between the ambassadors and other characters and visitors to the space station.

Additional major characters introduced in the pilot include Lieutenant Commander Laurel Takashima, Sinclair's second in command played by Tamlyn Tamito. Laurel oversees day-to-day operations from the command center. She was born on Earth.

CHIEF OF SECURITY

Jerry Doyle portrays recovering alcoholic Michael Garibaldi, the chief of security. Garibaldi bounced from assignment to assignment before Babylon 5.

Doyle, a former investment banker, turned to acting with some success. His previous work includes appearing as a guest star on MOONLIGHTING, REASONABLE DOUBTS, and THE BOLD AND THE BEAUTIFUL. He played in the recent films BEING IN TIME and KIDNAPPED. On the stage he's appeared in the plays "A Thousand Clowns," "The Country Girl," "Death Knocks," and "Rock-A-Bye Hamlet." When the initial BABYLON 5 two-hour pilot aired he could be seen in a McDonald's commercial.

Richard Compton directed the pilot of BABYLON 5 and several episodes. He feels Chief Garibaldi grows more interesting as the series progresses thanks to the script writers and series creator J. Michael Straczynski.

Patricia Tallman plays the station's resident telepath, Lyta Alexander. She monitors business deals.

Babylon 5's chief physician and xenobiologist, Dr. Benjamin Kyle, portrayed by Johnny Seka, rounds out the cast. Kyle works to create a definitive text on alien biology.

The last character in the original pilot was not planned to appear weekly. Blaire Baron plays Carolyn Sykes, a free merchant and captain of her own ship. Sinclair and Sykes rekindle their past relationship when she comes to Babylon 5.

Walter Koenig as a psy cop on an episode of BABLYON 5.

Photo ©1994 Warner Bros., Inc.

ORIGIN OF BABYLON 5

Veteran writer J. Michael Straczynski created BABYLON 5. Straczynski spent a lot of time in the science fiction genre. He previously wrote for CAPTAIN POWER AND THE SOLDIERS OF THE FUTURE and served as story editor and writer for the TWILIGHT ZONE syndicated series.

Straczynski wanted a show that would do for television science fiction what HILL STREET BLUES did for police dramas. He wanted well-developed characters and tight storylines, not flashy special effects.

He created BABYLON 5 knowing thus far only three kinds of science fiction shows have appeared on television. He calls one type the "in search of" stories. This type includes STAR TREK, BATTLESTAR GALACTICA, SPACE: 1999, and LOST IN SPACE. Each involves voyaging to a new world every week.

He dubs another type "the man on the run" stories. THE IMMORTAL,

STARMAN, QUESTOR TAPES, and THE INCREDIBLE HULK fall into this group.

Then there are the anthology shows.

BABYLON 5 falls under none of these convenient labels. Instead mainstream dramas inspired a permanent environment in which the stories come to the regular characters. A space station seemed to be the logical choice.

Straczynski wanted science fiction for adults. He says, "No kids or cute robots." He envisioned BABYLON 5 as a classic saga with a beginning and an end.

Straczynski wrote the treatment and writer's bible for BABYLON 5 in 1988. He then teamed up with executive producer Doug Netter, producer John Copeland, and story editor Lawrence DiTillio. The group had worked together on CAPTAIN POWER.

Copeland brought along special effects coordinator Ron Thornton, also from CAPTAIN POWER, and later the ADDAMS FAMILY and TERMINATOR 2.

INTRODUCTION: THE VIDEO TOASTER

Foundation Imaging, the company run by Ron Thornton, is located in Valencia, California, just north of Los Angeles. As the Special Effects Supervisor, he helps craft spaceships and other special space effects for BABYLON 5.

Thornton rejects the traditional route taken by STAR TREK, STAR WARS, and other space series. No "hard models" appear on BABYLON 5. Computers generate all the special effects.

Computer animation passed through its formative stages with TRON and THE LAST STARFIGHT-ER. They won an Emmy Award for the BABYLON 5's two-hour pilot film, "The Gathering."

Thornton began his career working in the special effects field in England on DR. WHO and BLAKE'S 7. He moved to Los Angeles for miniature work on CLASS OF 1999, THE ADDAMS FAMILY, HIGHLANDER 2, and TERMINATOR 2. While working on the TV series CAPTAIN POWER, Thornton learned to create effects on an Amiga computer.

That was still a developmental stage for computer effects. Later he found that the hardware had become capable of serious imaging.

When NewTek's Video Toaster hit the market, Thornton began to experiment with the possible. LightWave, a 3-D software program, uses the terminology of designers. This enabled Thornton's group to design models similar to traditional special effects.

For example, only one side is built for some models because only one side will be seen. If a model will only be seen from the front there is no point in building a back.

STATE OF THE ART EFFECTS

BABYLON 5 tripled the number of special effects shots after Thornton

showed the producers what he could do with a computer. Two hundred Vorlon fighters, transports, and motherships appear in "The Gathering." Industrial Light & Magic hasn't attempted anything that demanding since RETURN OF THE JEDI in 1983.

Computer lighting appears more interesting since spacecraft don't have to be brightly lit against the blackness of outer space. Vessels with shadowed areas look sharp.

ILM used 50 special effects technicians on STAR WARS. Foundation Imaging employs five people adding several more for post-production.

The high cost of special effects traditionally broke the backs of ambitious science fiction projects. BABYLON 5 stays within a reasonable budget. The effects cost half what they would have a decade ago. This may pave the way for future science fiction shows with off world settings.

With the basic production crew assembled, the producers began making the rounds. Traditional television networks resisted the series. Networks think men like adventure and women like soap operas. They find science fiction strange and uncomfortable.

The success of STAR TREK has had little impact on the networks. They don't think the show can be copied. The once top rated THE INCREDIBLE HULK was never imitated for the same reason.

SCI FI ON TELEVISION

Pitching a TV series involves entering a room full of strangers and explaining a concept. Joe Straczynski turned to artist Peter Ledger for help. He worked with Straczynski to conceptualize the Babylon 5 station.

A drawing helps an executive visualize a pitch. It clarifies strange concepts. This only works up to a point. As Larry DiTillio, the BABYLON 5 story editor, put it, "With network execs, a picture is worth ten words."

Science fiction shows also bring special budgetary worries due to complicated special effects. Networks worry about expenses. Previous producers have claimed they could create an inexpensive science fiction series then proved quite the opposite. They were stumbling blocks for BABYLON 5.

A lot of industry people didn't believe the show could be produced for a reasonable price. They'd already heard too many promises. Straczynski and company solved the problems before pitching their show.

SELLING THE SERIES

Straczynski pitched the concept to all three networks, HBO, and several others before presenting it to Chris-Craft Television. In 1989 Chris-Craft pledged support for BABYLON 5.

Its representative, Evan Thompson, stands firmly behind the series. Evan understood the concept while other executives failed to grasp the idea. Evan's enthusiasm helped keep up the spirits of Straczynski and his associates while they put together a production deal.

THE WARNER CONNECTION

After several attempts at co-production deals, BABYLON 5 went to Warner Brothers. Evan brought the project to Dick Roberts at Warner Domestic television. They put together the international co-venture that made the show possible. In 1991 BABYLON 5 became one of the three flagship programs on Warners' Prime Time Entertainment Network (PTEN).

CREATING THE GATHERING

Richard Compton directed the pilot for BABYLON 5, "The Gathering." Compton started out in television as an actor. In 1966 he met Gene Roddenberry during an airline flight. They struck up a conversation and Roddenberry gave Compton a chance to appear in an episode of STAR TREK. Compton played a member of Scotty's repair crew in "The Doomsday Machine."

He cut his teeth writing and directing low budget films for Roger Corman. Numerous television and feature film credits followed, including two MACON COUNTY LINE movies.

Twenty years after appearing on "The Doomsday Machine," Compton directed the NEXT GENERATION episode "Haven." He found the rules of the series too restrictive.

A few years later he jumped at the chance to direct the pilot of BABYLON 5. Compton enjoyed the opportunity but felt the episode aired lacked 20 minutes of material it needed.

He tried to get the script edited prior to filming. Series creator J. Michael Straczynski refused because it was too long.

At that point Compton wished he'd used the five days spent filming the deleted scenes shooting the footage used. After directing four episodes, he parted ways with the producers over the direction of the series.

AN OUTPOST IN SPACE

The two hour pilot aired in February 1993. It introduced viewers to "one lone outpost in space," dropping tantalizing hints of the mysteries that might unfold in the series. The BABYLON 5 pilot won the highest ratings of any Warner Brothers' Prime Time Entertainment Network premiere.

Although the BABYLON 5 pilot did well in the ratings, it got mixed reviews from fans and critics. The cutting edge computer special effects earned praise, and eventually an Emmy. Other than that, critics didn't like the show.

Many found the human characters pale and uninteresting compared to the alien ambassadors. Others complained about sets and costuming they felt buried the actors under too much make-up. Many found the plot uninspired.

Straczynski admits the pilot was "flawed" by production problems. The telefilm ran 20 minutes too long and had to be cut. "All the character stuff ended up on the cutting room floor," says Straczynski. Budget limitations forced the crew to rent many of the props used in the pilot.

BABYLON 5's ratings warranted a continuing series, but Warner Brothers dragged its feet making a final decision. In the interim, Straczynski and crew overhauled the shoENTER CLAUDIA

CHRISTIAN

Major cast changes included replacing almost all female cast members. Claudia Christian's Susan Ivanova replaced Laurel Takashima, played by Tamlyn Tamito.

Claudia's career began in an episode of the prime time soap DALLAS. She also appeared in THE HIDDEN, RELENTLESS, and CLEAN AND SOBER and the low budget films ARENA, MANIAC COP 2, and HEXED.

On television Claudia Christian played a recurring role on BLACK'S MAGIC, a series which only lasted a few episodes. She portrayed the former lover of the main character on SPACE RANGERS. Smaller roles include an episode of QUANTUM LEAP, L.A. LAW, MATLOCK, and MURDER SHE WROTE.

Patricia Tallman played the telepath Lyta Alexander for the pilot. Instead of Alexander, the series featured Andrea Thompson as Talia Winters, another telepath.

Sinclair got a new love interest in the form of Catherine Sakai, played by Julia Nickson. A younger actor, Richard Biggs, playing the part of Dr. Steven Franklin replaced Johnny Seka as Benjamin Kyle.

Production designs were also changed. They redid the Earth Alliance uniforms to give them more color, rebuilt sets, and constructed new props. Slight changes

appear in the alien ambassadors' make-up.

A FIVE YEAR MISSION

Warner Brothers committed to a 22 episode order a few months after the pilot aired. Filming started in mid-July of 1993. The weekly series premiered the week of January 22, 1994 with plans for a five year run.

The series' creator planned a five year arc of stories in which the show progresses and changes over time. Alliances change. Loyalties change. Characters undergo change. Some live while others die. Creator Straczynski sees it as a five year mini-series.

The producers want to portray science differently than other TV shows set in outer space. For example, for the first time on television, there is no sound in the vacuum of space.

The center of the space station is called the Garden. It contains farm land inside a self-sustaining environment. They portray this enclosed environment in space with great scientific accuracy.

As of this writing a little bit over half of the first season's episodes have aired. Unlike the usual television series, BABYLON 5 runs from January through December. They held back the final first run episodes for the November ratings period.

The first season of BABYLON 5 shows varying episode quality. High points include "The Parliament of Dreams," "The Believers," and "And The Sky Full of Stars." These episodes offer interesting stories and good visual effects. The low end of the spectrum includes "Infection," a hackneyed tale of bio-weaponry, and the mediocre "Soul Hunter."

THE STYLE OF THE STORIES

BABYLON 5 failed to rid itself of the problems in the pilot. The flamboyant ambassadors G'Kar and Lando steal scenes and make the human crew look pale by comparison.

Luckily, human characters appear in many scenes by themselves, allowing for development. The uniforms still look too dark and carry little ornamentation. Many sets seem unnecessarily dark.

BABYLON 5, the first show to totally employ computer generated effects instead of models, delivers stunning images. Every episode tops what came before. Even more spectacular effects will appear at the end of the season.

Despite initial comparisons to DEEP SPACE NINE, BABYLON 5 is very different. BABYLON 5 works best when it is the least like STAR TREK.

Good examples include the episodes "Midnight on the Firing Line" and "Believers." "Midnight on the Firing Line" deals with military and political complexities in a more realistic manner than STAR TREK. "The Believers" confronts issues of morality and cultural relativism, themes not unknown to STAR TREK—THE NEXT GENERATION, but with an ending unlike any other program.

CASTING CHANGE

In the future, series lead Michael O'Hare will be replaced. Warner Brothers renewed BABYLON 5 for a second season, but insisted O'Hare be replaced. The studio feels he lacks screen presence. Unfortunately Straczynski conceived O'Hare as the pivotal character in the series.

BABYLON 5 presents an intriguing universe and interesting characters. The potential of the series has not been realized. The creative team now facies the problems of getting a new show off the ground.

Certainly better things will come in the future. Though not unflawed, BABYLON 5 has made a good showing. Its place in the annals of sci-fi television history will be determined by what follows.

Some of the more unusual aliens regularly seen on BABYLON 5.

Photo ©1994 Warner Bros., Inc.

William Shatner as Bascom, the mysterious head of the security company which works behind the scenes on TEKWAR.

Several years ago William Shatner realized that STAR TREK, the vehicle that made him, wasn't his to control. Its spin-offs left him behind. So he came up with a sci fi series to build into his own mini-empire.

TEKWAR

William Shatner's TEK books began appearing in 1991. Their commercial success meant that a film or TV adaptation would follow close behind.

TEKWAR fills a successful place in Universal Television's ACTIONPACK series of TV movies, also including HERCULES, MIDNIGHT RUN, and others. It gets its own regular slot in the Fall.

William Shatner and Ron Goulart write the novels. The first two novels may have already been written by Goulart before Shatner heard of the project.

Atlantis Films of Toronto optioned the novels in the summer of 1992. The company has produced TV shows for 15 years, including RAY BRADBURY THEATRE.

Jeremey Katz, a vice-president of Atlantis Films, knew the TEKWAR needed more funding than they could give. They sought out a partner and made a deal with Universal's MCA TV division.

MCA was assembling a package of 24 made for TV movies. TEKWAR fit perfectly, and Universal has plenty of money.

The premise of the series puts policeman Jake Cardigan, played by Greg Evigan, into jail. He supposedly sold out to the Teklords, resulting in the deaths of his partners. His sentence runs 15 years in Cryosleep, a suspended animation process.

Four years later someone revives and releases him, although he doesn't know whom. Jake finds that his wife remarried and took their now 15 year old son with her. She hid her trail. Only Bascom, played by William Shatner, believes Jake is innocent.

T.J. AND THE TEKLORDS

The novels make Jake Cardigan a middle-aged man. Shatner describes him as a T.J. Hooker in the future.

The TV series shaves a few years off Jake's age. He's now in his mid-thirties.

Shatner supported casting Greg Evigan in the role. "Modeled on Greg, Jake is younger, handsomer and less gritty than imagined before. Among all the other people we wanted to cast, I wanted Greg. His quality is more gregarious than angry. So it made sense to write it for him," says Shatner.

Greg Evigan's career ran a low profile career for several years. His feature work includes the films DEEP STAR SIX and STRIPPED TO KILL. On television he starred in B.J. AND THE BEAR a decade ago and more recently in the sitcom MY TWO DADS. Evigan describes Jake Cardigan, saying, "We're both more concerned with doing what's right than with acquiring wealth and power."

After awakening, Jake asks about his 11 year old son. The man says Danny is now fifteen.

Jake's released on parole and given 1500 credits. He goes to his old house, which his wife kept in his name when she filed for divorce. This contemporary Toronto house looks familiar to TV audiences.

THE WAR OVER TEK

Jake encounters one of his old partners, Sid

Gomez, played by Eugene Clark. He now works for Cosmos Security, a company owned and run by Bascom.

The influential Bascom helped make Cuba the 51st state. The films reveal only one or two items about the future, not enough to shape the world of 2040.

Bascom agrees to help Jake clear his name. In return Cardigan must work for him, helping to find a missing scientist, Prof. Kittridge. The scientist previously worked on a device to neutralize Tek.

Tek is addictive and illegal. Users wear the device which generates hallucinations more realistic than virtual reality. Since a user achieves any fantasy, many stop at nothing to maintain their fix.

This show never addresses important questions. If Tek becomes psychologically addictive couldn't the addict stay in the illusionary state long enough to starve to death? Wouldn't there be a market for longer lasting and more powerful Tek chips? Good science fiction answers questions like these.

VIRTUAL REALITY

Tek seems inspired by the original STAR TREK episode "The Menagerie." It presented an alien race addicted to hallucinations. The aliens allow their civilization to crumble. The United Federation of Planets quarantines the planet under penalty of death. Tek applies the idea to a world of computer technology and virtual reality.

The future may bring Tek, but virtual reality promises far more than it delivers. Virtual reality merely tricks the eye, and prolonged use even causes eyestrain. Computer technology magazines such as WIRED report the problems. Of course, these problems may disappear over time.

TEKWAR takes place when virtual reality has been perfected, 50 years from now. The novels place it 200 years in the future, but the TV people feared viewers wouldn't relate to such a distant future. More likely the difficulties of filming.

Greg Evigan as Jake Cardigan, the star of TEKWAR.
Photo ©1994 The Lippin Group

ANDROIDS WITH A MISSION

TEKWAR introduces humanoid robots called "sims." The robots take offense if called "mechs."

The first robot Jake meets, a little girl, grabs a woman Cardigan needs to meet to get information about Prof. Kittridge. The robot blows itself up, killing the informant. It later turns out the informant was also a robot.

Jake goes to Prof. Kittridge's secret lab. He finds the Prof.'s daughter in cryosleep. She's actually an android in the image of Beth Kittridge.

The android reveals that her programming requires her to protect Beth Kittridge and that she carries Beth's memories. When they seemingly discover Beth murdered, the android unblocks memories which apply to Jake.

Apparently Beth Kittridge witnessed Jake's kidnapping and brainwashing. The kidnappers left Jake to die from an overdose of Tek but Beth saved his brain from being fried. It left him seeming like a Tek addict coming down off a high. Beth glimpsed the real culprit.

The Beth Kittridge android, called L-10, falls in love with Jake. She ultimately sacrifices herself to protect Jake from an android of his son. The boy android blows up, destroying L-10.

AND THE KILLER IS. . .

TEKWAR introduces a "morph mask." It simulates anyone's face.

People sometimes detect errors in the masks. These give the wearer away.

The waterfront headquarters of teklord Sonny Hakori possesses an invisibility screen. A person must step through to learn it is there.

In the climax, the traitor who framed Jake is revealed to be a police mech. When the robot lays dying, it refuses to reveal its programmer. This leaves the end hanging and allows TEKLORDS to follow TEKWAR.

The first film faithfully followed the first novel. Subsequent films stray further afield.

Jake's relationship with his ex-wife and son remain unresolved in TEKWAR. After he is cleared of the crime his family don't hate him any more but still don't want to live with him. This is resolved in the second film, .

THE FATE OF SONNY

HAKORI

Sonny Hakori is arrested in TEKWAR, is now in prison. A computer virus he helped create attacks people and puts them in a coma in TEKLORDS. An investigator falls victim and dies.

Jake and his son, Danny, endure a strained relationship in TEKWAR. They make up in TEK LORDS.

Jake admits that when he was a policeman he ignored his son. Jake listens when Kate, his ex-wife, calls Danny. Before Jake and Danny arrive at her house, the computer virus attacks her. Jake rushes her to the hospital.

At the hospital, Kate's new husband, Bennett, attacks Jake. He tries to blame Jake for what happened to Kate.

This convincing emotional sceneleads to the climax of the film. The conclusion reveals Bennettas being in partnership with Sonny Hatori and the Teklords.

Kate had been calling to tell Jake when Bennett tried to kill her with the virus. This conveniently kicks Bennett out of the picture so Jake can begin a rapprochement with his wife and son.

It would have been more interesting if Bennett had been a good, decent man. Then Jake would face the dilemma of knowing that his wife and child had a good home. With Bennett exposed as a criminal, Jake's life resumes its course.

Saving Kate provides a happy ending. TEKLORDS fails to compel. The most interesting element is the hologram of Sonny's sister, who had been killed in an assassination attempt on Sonny. She survived by having her mind transferred into a computer. It turns out Sonny set his sister up so she kills him and destroys herself in the climax.

HEIR TO THE THRONE

TEKLAB takes place in England. The heir to the throne of Great Britain goes into hiding because the royal family was overthrown.

The people of England love the royal family. Even the Irish Republican Army won't harm them. Devastating reprisals followed the IRA attack on a royal yacht 15 years ago.

The royal family forms an important part of the character and self-esteem of the British people. Their power granted comes only from the British Parliament.

The producers of TEKLAB went to London with the director, Timothy Bond. They took many pictures then returned to shoot in Toronto as a stand-in for London. To complete the illusion, mattes of famous London landmarks were matted into the background on the film. Timothy Bond previously directed episodes of STAR TREK—THE NEXT GENERATION and WAR OF THE WORLDS, and the LOST WORLD miniseries, a project yet to surface in America.

TEK DIRECTORS

Greg Evigan compared directors on the first three

TEKWAR films for SCIENCE FICTION AGE, saying, "With any director, all the excitement is in the beginning. You both want to bring to the table what you've got and neither of you knows what that is. By the end you know each other very well and you're ready for something new.

"On TEKWAR," he continued, "Bill was excited. He really wanted to do the project and that gave him an incredible amount of energy. He always knew what he wanted, and because he's an actor, he understood our needs.

"George Bloomfield, on TEKLORDS, admitted he didn't know a thing about the technical part of what we were doing, so he was all about the relationships between the actors and he had a certain style with lenses: lots of extreme close-ups where you could see the pores and what's behind the eyes."

He concluded, saying, "Tim (Bond) is very open to working things out on the spot, ad-libbing and trying to add to what the writer wrote. It's a freer style—personally, I like it a lot."

DESIGNING THE FUTURE

Producer and art director Stephen Roloff read the original novels to pick futuristic settings for filming. Shatner gave Roloff carte blanche. He told him to take what he wanted and leave the rest.

Roloff wanted to ground the series in a recognizable reality while enhancing imaginative elements. He moved TEKWAR from 200 years in the future to only 50. The series also moves the orbital cryosleep prison to Earth.

"If an image has something very futuristic right beside something very old, that will always make the futuristic element look that much more hi-tech," Roloff says. "Usually, on TV you just tear the guts out of things, computer bits, pipes, and things and glue them to the wall. We won't be having that BLADE RUNNER wet neon look, which is very sexy. That would be a direct rip-off."

Although location work shot in Vancouver and Toronto, they used impressive standing sets, particularly the central command office of the Cosmos Detective Agency. The large standing set includes both the building exterior and huge interiors with transparent floor panels, glass walls, and computer screens.

ENTER CYBERSPACE

The futuristic designs of TEKWAR began with the concepts of Archigram, a British company developing "clip-on, plug-in" architecture. Ideas in progress today will reach fruition in the decades to come when TEKWAR takes place.

The idea that computers can be changed by pulling out old pieces and plugging in new ones lies behind the plug-in, clip-on technology. They call it modular housing.

Other futuristic touches in the series include walls that change from opaque to transparent at the touch of a button. Viewers relate to these new devices that lie just over the hill.

In TEKWAR people access a visible cyberspace. Roloff says, "Creating a cyberspace with a visual matrix seemed like a good notion for a detective."

Jake Cardigan receives visual feedback from what he accesses in the global cyberspace network. He wears a device on his head to directly connect to the computer system. The style of computer animation looks very '90s.

STYLES OF SPECIAL EFFECTS

Stephen Roloff doesn't like the look of Computer animation. He cites BABYLON 5 as an example of what can go wrong. He says, "Whenever they cut to the outside world, it was like cutting to Toontown," a reference to the cartoon world seen in WHO

FRAMED ROGER RAB- BIT. He feels the special effects on BABYLON 5 look too neat and pristine compared to the dark grit- ty realism of live action segments.

The cyberspace on TEKWAR isn't supposed to look familiar with. It can be imaginative and stylis- tic.

Roloff also objects that computer animation is done by few technicians while live action filming involves the ideas of many people. He says, "I can't believe that one person sit- ting alone at a computer can possibly match that mass creativity."

TEKWAR uses a variety of special effects tech- niques based on what best achieves the look.

Not everything futuris- tic needs complicated spe- cial effects. One back- ground effect, the "Adway," encloses streets papered with advertising cars travel on. Since the production company lacks a backlot and budget for futuristic cars, they use the enclosed highway.

Unlike the futuristic cars driven in BLADE RUNNER and other films, Jake Cardigan drives a Jeep, supposedly a classic 1999 model. A futuristic police van is a shell built on top of another car.

THREADS OF THE FUTURE

Sherry McMorran designs the costuming for TEKWAR. She previously worked on CAPTAIN POWER.

The art director wanted a sophisticated, colorful jumble of designs from dif- ferent eras, avoiding the cliché of skin tight suits. In this future society has become a melting pot of different cultures.

The uniforms of police, nurses, paramedics, and the like would also be col- orful not drab as in the '90s. Paramedics dress in bright blue; nurses wear gold uniforms.

Night scenes help TEK- WAR look futuristic. Little elements such as a ultra- modern phone booths add a special touch. Despite night scenes and Tek addiction, TEKWAR por- trays a bright future.

This future includes forests where people live voluntarily cut off from normal society. The first TEKWAR film presents Warbride, played by Sheena Easton as a radical environmentalist leading like minded people. Warbride takes her name from her vow to wed herself only to the fight to save the Earth.

TEKWORLD

TEKWAR is part of the ACTION PACK from Universal Television. Action must fill the stories. Shatner says , "The secret behind shooting action is a good location that allows you to be cinematic about the action," something Shatner was very concerned with when he directed the pilot episode. "Action-adventure is like a flickering fire. I've never quite understood why people watch a flickering fire, but we all do. I think the appeal has something to do with what action is, people running and jumping and shooting and hitting. The eye is drawn to it."

Shatner encountered a hazard of directing when Evigan's eyes were burned in a scene hospitalizing him for two days. Shatner used Evigan's double and shot around the missing performer. Luckily the injuries were not severe and he quickly returned to filming.

William Shatner makes cameo appearances in the TEKWAR series as Bascom, the head of the Cosmos Detective Agency. He serves as a unifying feature in the four films thus far, TEKWAR, TEK-LORDS, TEKLAB, and TEK JUSTICE.

A regular TEKWAR series joins the line-up of syndicated adventure shows in the Fall of 1994. Twenty four episodes will air, the same number as HIGHLANDER and ROBOCOP, the two other Toronto based science fiction series. TEKWAR fills the vacancy left by TIME TRAX.

This series premiered in January 1993, the same month as DEEP SPACE NINE. The series failed to build an audience and so it died in May 1993, the first casualty of the new sci fi television boom.

TIME TRAX: THE END OF THE HUNT

Time travel remained a popular staple of science fiction since H.G. Wells wrote his oft reprinted novel THE TIME MACHINE a century ago. The concept appeared in motion pictures for more than 60 years. TV appearances trace back to an early episode of the 1950s THE ADVENTURES OF SUPERMAN series.

In the 1960s Irwin Allen built an entire TV series around the idea, THE TIME TUNNEL. It lasted one year. A similar fate befell TIME TRAX after 16 months.

Easy parallels connect TIME TRAX and THE TIME TUNNEL. Both use time travel as a gimmick interesting enough to relegate everything else to secondary importance.

Instead of using time travel as the basis for dramatic adventures, TIME TRAX fell back on standard plots. Darien Lambert gets into scrapes rather than confronting the larger issues time travel raises.

The producers claimed the show wouldn't be cops and robbers. This is exactly what it became.

Darien Lambert (Dale Midkiff) of TIME TRAX.
Photo ©1994 Lorimar Television

The two hour pilot episode of TIME TRAX begins in the year 2193. A villain, Mordicai Sahmbi, played by Peter Donat, invents a time machine in the basement of the Smithsonian Institute. Sahmbi wants to enrich himself by helping wanted criminals escape 200 years into the past, the limit of the time machine's operating parameters.

DEADLY ESCAPE

Dr. Sahmbi tries to woo his assistant, Elissa, played by Mia Sara. Instead she hits it off with police detective Darien Lambert, portrayed by Dale Midkiff.

The bright young detective is stymied by the number of wanted fugitives who seemingly disappear. Darien meets Elissa when he follows a criminal into the neighborhood of the Smithsonian.

Darien's suspicions and Elissa's knowledge of Dr. Sahmbi's experiments lead them to deduce the answer. The cornered scientist uses the machine to project himself into the past.

When Elissa refuses to come with him, he kills her before Darien's eyes. Darien vows to go after Sahmbi and track down the missing criminals. Since a person can only safely make one round trip through time, a returned criminal cannot escape into the past again.

Darien brings a pocket computer named "Selma." It is disguised to look like a credit card. Selma sometimes only appears as a voice, other times as a hologram in the form of a middle-aged woman played by Elizabeth Alexander.

DOSSIER ON DALE MIDKIFF

The pilot offers an interesting relationship between Darien and a female Secret Service agent. She should have remained part of the team throughout the series, but was dropped in because of Selma.

Dale Midkiff plays Darien Lambert. He comes across flat and restrained. The typical bland hero fails to capture viewer interest. By trying to create someone everyone could relate to, they created a character that remains distant and uninvolved.

Midkiff previously starred in the motion picture PET SEMATARY and played Elvis Presly on TV. He also appeared in the short-lived TV series DREAM STREET and the low budget film LOVE POTION NO. 9.

BACKGROUND ON DR. SAHMBI

Character actor Peter Donat portrays recurring villain Dr. Mordicai Sahmbi. The nephew of Robert Donat has an extensive list of screen credits, including the films THE GODFATHER PART II, THE HINDENBERG, BILLY JACK GOES TO WASHINGTON, THE WAR OF THE ROSES, and TUCKER. He guest-starred on many TV series and co-starred in TV mini-series including THE CAPTAINS AND THE KINGS,

THE NEW SCI FI TV BOOK

RICH MAN, POOR MAN BOOK II, THE LINDBERGH KIDNAPPING CASE, and THE MISSILES OF OCTOBER.

Little is revealed of the background of Dr. Sahmbi. Instead, the actor made up his own. He speculates that Mordicai had a Tibetan father and an English mother and spent time in India before being educated at Oxford, Cambridge, and other schools around the world.

THE TREK CONNECTION

TIME TRAX filmed in Australia due to Lorimar's low budget of $730,000 per episode. The series spent half what it costs to film a one hour show in the United States.

The production team on TIME TRAX included Gary Nardino, Grant Rosenberg, Jeffrey Hayes, and Harve Bennett. All previously worked together at Paramount Studios on STAR TREK motion pictures.

Bennett produced STAR TREK II through STAR TREK V, leaving the series when Paramount turned down his idea for STAR TREK VI. He became involved in TIME TRAX when contacted by Gary Nardino.

Nardino told him Lorimar wanted a syndicated series but needed ideas. The four producers discussed different ideas. They finally pitched one for a detective from 200 years in the future who goes into his past chasing fugitives.

They essentially packaged a reversal of the classic THE FUGITIVE TV series. Instead of a man fleeing the police, they told the story of a policeman chasing fugitives.

SHOT DOWN

TIME TRAX offered a variety of plots. The producers didn't want much science on the show. They hired writers inexperienced at science fiction. Scripts often followed TV formulas.

Standard scripts included a child abuse episode ("The Prodigy"), an episode about a man with a son missing in action in Southeast Asia, a story about an evil twin, and even an episode about a star stalker. The fan from the future stalks a woman in 1994 before she becomes a successful singer.

Another cliché episode centers on boxing ("The Contender"). A man from the future, when boxing is outlawed, goes into the past to become a professional boxer. Since everyone in the future is smarter, faster, and stronger than 20th Century humans, he has an unfair advantage. The story centers on whether it was right for him to use this advantage than on whether boxing deserved to be banned.

The series explored some science fiction ideas. They didn't worry whether changes in the past would affect the future. One theory said that Dr. Sahmbi's time machine sent people into a parallel world not their actual past. The second season proved to be the last.

This is the wild card in the pack. The show plays to a different part of the marketplace. It may be the most popular of them all as the number one children's show in the country. It's an unqualified hit for the Fox Network.

MIGHTY MORPHIN POWER RANGERS

On Monday February 21st, 1994, the Hollywood Freeway turned into a parking lot for an eight mile long traffic jam. The cause? 35,000 people, primarily pre-teen children and their parents, trying to get into Universal Studios Hollywood. They wanted to see the first public appearance of the actors who portray The Mighty Morphin Power Rangers.

Thousands were turned away because the arena where the Power Rangers appeared couldn't hold so many. Never before had crowds descended on Universal Studios in such numbers.

The reaction to the appearance of the entire cast of DEEP SPACE NINE at Universal Studios Hollywood had been far more sedate. On that Saturday, just three months before, only about 800 people turned out.

No traffic jams. No horde of screaming fans. Just the usual reaction in Hollywood to the appearance of TV stars.

Three months later, the young fans of THE MIGHTY MORPHIN POWER RANGES set a new precedent the way only wild-eyed kids can. No self-respecting adult science fiction show operates at this manic pace.

The show is a part of the Fox Children's Network. The live action adventure about teenagers who transform themselves into superheroes caught on big time.

Proof of that was established beyond any doubt in December 1993 when toy stores sold out of the Mighty Morphin Power Rangers toys the day they were delivered. Parents lined up waiting to purchase them. This phenomenon continues even though the Christmas season is months in the past.

The TV show airs six days a week. It is the highest rated children's show in the country.

The Rangers have been compared with the Ninja Turtles since they both came out of nowhere to top the popularity charts. Saban Entertainment, which produces the American version of POWER RANGERS, is already being courted by movie studios.

MIGHTY MORPHIN POWER RANGERS debuted in September 1993. Unlike the other new sci fi series, this one already capitalizes on its instant popularity by releasing half-hour episodes on home video.

ORIGINS OF THE POWER RANGERS

Saban Entertainment based their version of MIGHTY MORPHIN POWER RANGERS on a Japanese science fiction series. Several years ago, a version of the series called DYNAMAN appeared on American television. It lasted only five syndicated tryout episodes.

DYNAMAN gives a group of Japanese young people the power to turn into superheroes. They summon various craft which assemble into one giant robot similar to the Transformers and similar toys.

Producing DYNAMAN follows the path Woody Allen blazed 20 years before in the movie WHAT'S UP TIGER LILY? Allen took a Japanese spy movie, dubbed it into English, and crafted a completely new storyline and entirely different dialogue. It emerged as a very funny parody of spy movies.

The producers of DYNAMAN used fantastic visuals to produce a funny science fiction satire, especially "The Lizard of Oz" episode. They spout such lines as, "Power to the police state! Right on!" after defeating a monster. by Gideon Brower and Shari Roman wrote and directed the hoot and a half.

Haim Saban saw the original Japanese version nine years ago. He bought the American distribution rights and tried to package it for U.S. networks. "In my mind I'm thinking that if I like it, then maybe other people will like it in America," he told an interviewer from the Fox affiliate in Los Angeles. "But I was wrong for nine years."

The failure of DYNAMAN paved the path for THE MIGHTY MORPHIN POWER RANGERS. They shot new footage for this version featuring American actors. Then they intercut the new footage with existing Japanese footage of the characters in costume.

They even reshot some of the fight scenes to include scenes of the actors in their street clothes. The original version includes very few scenes in civilian attire.

A HOT HIT FOR FOX

Margaret Loesch, the president of the Fox Children's Network, recognized the potential when it was brought to her. "When I first saw it, I loved it," she says.

Not all affiliates which carry the Fox Children's Network originally agreed to run this strange action adventure show for kids. Loesch reveals, "They thought it was abominable."

She feels the show's popularity comes from appealing to both girls and boys. Loesch told the L.A. TIMES, "Ultimately I think that it is maybe every child's dream to be able to metamorphosize into a super hero and beat the bad guy.

"Kids are desperately in need of positive role models and, whether or not they like the show, people agree that our teenage stars are delightful to both boys and girls," she says, "and it is extremely rare that an action-adventure show appeals to girls as well as boys."

Some people object to the violence of this successful action series which appeals to children. It is hard to call fighting space aliens, robots, and monsters violence as we understand it.

As Shuki Levy puts it, "It's all relative. You can go back to the Bible stories and say maybe children shouldn't hear about David slaying Goliath. Here we have only imaginary monsters and you see them making it out of clay in a machine. So you never feel like they have killed a real person or an animal. In the other side of the story, you never see the Rangers fighting other people, and I think it's easy for kids to see the difference."

MULTI-CULTURAL HEROES

The show stars Austin St. John as Jason, The Dragon Zord, Thuy Trang as Trini, the Griffin, Walter Jones as Zack, the Lion, Amy Jo Johnson as Kimberly, The Fire Bird, and David Yost as Billy, the Griffin. The multi-cultural group includes two girls and three boys.

One boy is Black and one girl is Asian. They symbolize the diversity of America, although all were Japanese in the original version. It shows an interesting difference in the societies behind the two series.

Costumes cover the actors entire heads. This conceals the identity of the person under the mask.

The producers stretch credibility by having two female characters while the original Japanese version has only one. When a female character transforms herself into a Power Ranger, her chest flattens all of a sudden.

The show also co-stars Paul Schrier as Bulk and Jason Narvy as Skull. The very fat Bulk and nerdy Skull add an odd message. They provide comedy relief. Bulk always looks ridiculous, making the show Politically inCorrect.

Executive producer Shuki Levy stated in an interview in the LOS ANGELES TIMES, "I'd be lying if I said we expected it to be like this, this big. It's incredible. It's crazy. But we always knew it had appeal for children, and that's because we have created this whole fantasy world with a somewhat primitive approach."

CAN'T WE ALL JUST TRY TO GET ALONG?

Most kids shows deliver morals. This series offers little sermons about getting along with others and not disliking someone just because they're different.

Fox anticipated the critics. At the end of some episodes they deliver an anti-violence disclaimer to the young viewers of the show.

"They may be getting subtle messages from the show," Loesch admits, "but these spots are not subtle and not confusing. They explain that the show is entertainment and what the kids should be learning are the values of the heroes and that they absolutely should not try to imitate the action."

A few days after their report on the popularity of the POWER RANGERS, the L.A. TIMES published a letter from three researchers in the Department of Child Development at Cal State Fullerton. They stated that their research indicates that young children who had just watched an episode of POWER RANGERS displayed six times the number of aggressive acts as a group of children who hadn't watched the episode. This shows that children learn more from what they see than what they are told.

Despite the Fox's claim, episodes in early June 1994 delivered no specific anti-violence message. Perhaps some local affiliates make room for extra commercials.

One episode showed a segment telling kids that

they should find a way to settle their differences without fighting. This isn't the same as telling viewers not to imitate the flying kicks of the Power Rangers.

RITA REPULSA

Queen Rita Repulsa, the main villain, looks like a '90s version of the Wicked Witch of the West. Trapped in a satellite prison, she escapes after 10,000 years and chooses to menace Earth.

An alien holographic head named Zordon gathers "Five teenagers with attitudes" to become the Power Rangers. They utter magic words to morph into colorful superheroes, shouting out names such as "Pterodactyl!" and "Saber Tooth!" When Zack changes into a Power Ranger he yells "Mastodon!"

The POWER RANGERS toys from Bandai America feature standard action figures, monsters and transforming zord robots. The White Tigerzord robot looks like a tiger and the zord robots interlock to create ultra zords and megazords.

THE MYSTERIOUS APPEAL

What is the appeal of the show? Even kids find it difficult to put it into words. When the young fans lined up at Universal Studios to see their heroes, they were interviewed by a local TV station. One nine year old boy tried to explain his fascination with the characters by saying, "I like Power Rangers because they fight and they never say bad languages."

Proving their appeal crosses the gender gap, a little girl said she likes the Power Rangers because, "They fight the crime and they're just cool."

So the next time a crime wave involving fifty foot monsters breaks out, you'll know who to call.

The NEXT GENERATION is gone. SEAQUEST is to be totally changed. VOYAGER airs for the first time. Just what surprises does the future hold for the most imaginative television genre?

by W.D. Kilpack III and James Van Hise

THE FUTURE OF SCIENCE FICTION ON TELEVISION

Where does a sci fan go after the departure of STAR TREK—THE NEXT GENER-ATION from television? That all depends.

Perhaps DEEP SPACE NINE is the safest place to go. The stories are grittier than NEXT GENERATION, more like the original STAR TREK. The special effects are excellent.

DEEP SPACE NINE is currently the second most popular one-hour syndicated drama, with over 15 million weekly watchers. With 48 episodes already in the can this show is finding itself and establishing a direction for the future. It will soon be the only first run STAR TREK on the air.

STAR TREK—VOYAGER

Paramount still hides their cards on STAR TREK—VOYAGER. It will involve a Starfleet vessel named The Voyager pursuing a Maquis ship, the rebels introduced on DEEP SPACE NINE andvseen in the NEXT GENERATION episode "Preemptive Strike."

Both ships slip into an uncharted wormhole and spit out in another galaxy hundreds of lightyears from home. The crews decide to join forces to try to get home. They also explore the new quadrant of space.

Unofficial but persistent rumors insist the Starfleet captain will be a woman, a "Lindsay Wagner" type. The same sources indicate both Jonathan Frakes and Marina Sirtis wanted to be on VOYAGER but Paramount wanted to start an entirely new cast.

The seventh season NEXT GENERATION episode "Lower Decks" introduced intriguing new characters. Rumors indicate that some of these characters may be featured in STAR TREK—VOYAGER series. Other sources deny this, but when did an episode of NEXT GENERATION last introduce several new crew members and focus primarily on them to the virtual exclusion of all regulars?

This series kicks off January 1995.

BABYLON 5

The second best new science fiction series drew an audience of 13.9 million for its pilot. It also won an Emmy Award.

Set on a space station at the galaxy's edge, the show bears superficial resemblance to DEEP SPACE NINE. BABYLON 5 lacks the budget Paramount gives science fiction shows.

State of the art computer effects impress audiences. The show strives for a different look from DEEP SPACE NINE and NEXT GENERATION.

The interior of Babylon 5 seems like a rat's warren of corridors, passageways, and rooms. There's no sense of where things begin or what they lead to. It would be interesting to track the characters from the command center down corridors to other areas to gain a better feel for the inside.

Some episodes offer A plots and B plots. The B plot often only provides an excuse for a space battle. The episode written by David Gerrold offers a prime example.

This is a pretty good show.

TEKWAR

The Trekker element starts with William Shatner. He not only co-writes the books, he plays a starring role and serves as executive producer of the series. He even occasionally sits in the director's chair.

Current plans call for four two-hour syndicated feature movies. It will become a weekly series in the Fall of 1994.

The stories mix cyberpunk with cops-and-robbers, BLADE RUNNER style, but with an opti-mistic view of the future—a big part of the success of the other STAR TREK series.

The movies fall short of the excellent books. The first followed the book and worked best. Later episodes lost the continuity of storyline, and forgot the novels!

For a Trekker fix, TEK-WAR started out strong but is petering out. Keep changing the channel.

TIME TRAX

Rated 43rd in popularity last season, this fails to capture Trekker power. TIME TRAX offers one attraction: a holographic British woman computer. She adds a touch of Data's android charm and Spock's logic, but a constantly rehashed storyline traps her.

Every episode follows the same plot: Cop learns a fleeing fugitive threatens to change the past and fixes the problem. The same basic story as QUANTUM LEAP, right down to the holographic friend. Aside from that obvious similarity, TRAX uses old plots previously seen on shows such as WILDERNESS FAMILY and the weekly series LOGAN'S RUN.

The series rapidly went downhill after the pilot. It's gone now.

Trekker fix? Not much. Next. . .

SEAQUEST DSV

Big names, led by Roy Scheider, a big ship (actually a submarine), a crisp original storyline, and a talking dolphin help make this a good show. It offers good special effects and good writing. Yet last year it ranked 79th in the ratings and shows little chance for improvement.

Like all three TREK series, SEAQUEST presents an optimistic view of the future, but it's Earthbound. The program goes under the waves not out to the stars.

Trekker fix? No, but worth watching. Renewed for a second season in its old Sunday night time slot on NBC.

ROBOCOP

Another sci fi series set on Earth. This one seems set in the same time period as SEAQUEST, but if this is the future I'd just as soon live in a submarine under the south Atlantic.

ROBOCOP offers a pessimistic view of the future. Technological marvels bring a dark side with every advance. Poverty and crime plague Old Detroit in the shadow of sparkling Delta City.

No one understands why the cyborg Robocop works while his predecessors malfunctioned. There may never be another.

The Chairman of OCP is a good man, but the people working for him have no ethics. Dr. Cray Z. Mallardo's discoveries continue to wreck havoc. The diet pill NoGain proved ragingly addictive.

The show offers a policeman's view of a world filled with crime and violence. ROBOCOP: THE SERIES provides a cautionary tale.

Sharp satire plays an important role in the show. The future doesn't look much different from our present. Current problems are magnified not solved.

SEAQUEST offers hope. ROBOCOP despairs, but entertains. Just don't think too much about the implications.

HIGHLANDER

This science fiction strays into fantasy. Spun off from the British motion picture series, it presents the story of immortals living among mankind.

A person's reaction to learning they will live forever unless beheaded reveals much. Some turn selfish or vainglorious while others seek learning.

Christopher Lambert plays Connor MacLeod, the protagonist in the movies. The TV series shifts the focus to his kinsman, Duncan MacLeod. Lambert only appeared in the pilot.

Other immortals want to kill Duncan MacLeod. The show avoids turing into the beheading of the week as characters explore their lives. The series continues the tradition of the first HIGHLANDER movie by using flashbacks to earlier points in MacLeod's life.

The second season introduced the society of The Watchers, mortals sworn to hunt down and kill all immortals. The show developed a strong fan following and the Queen music of the soundtrack really kicks butt, unlike the sedate soundtracks of most TV series.

Viewers wait to see what star Adrian Paul does after HIGHLANDER runs its course.

LOIS & CLARK

A series about a man from another planet with powers and abilities far beyond those of mortal men is science fiction. A superman among ordinary men appeared in science fiction many times. Superman is the most visible.

This series presents strong dramatic moments and more good comedy than any of the other shows. The series centers on Lois and Clark, just as the title implies.

This is an ensemble show. Perry White and Jimmy Olsen are strong characters.

The Daily Planet acts as the focal point for each episode. Stories spin out from there.

Dean Cain portrays Clark Kent/Superman as very likable with definite star quality. Teri Hatcher shows a flare for light comedy as Lois Lane. She demonstrates a good range of acting techniques.

Budget requirements restrict the number of special effects so Superman appears less than in the movies. The entertaining show offers a different Superman than ever seen on film before.

POWER RANGERS

Special effects footage from a Japanese science fiction show combines with new footage of a racially balanced crew of high school kids for this popular series. The kids turn into the Power Rangers.

This fast paced, hard driving science fiction action show offers wild stunts and wilder characters, including huge robots and giant monsters. When the American actors who portray the Power Rangers made a personal appearance at Universal Studios Hollywood early in 1994, thirty thousand people turned out causing massive traffic jams.

Power Rangers toys remain popular and difficult to find. Stores can't keep them on the shelves!

BEYOND THE HORIZON?

NBC/Spielberg plans a new project called EARTH 2. In the series, man first colonizes an alien planet. The series begins next fall.

The Trek franchise offers a fourth series, STAR TREK—VOYAGER, scheduled to debut in January 1995 on Paramount's new network. The program promises new aliens in a previously unrevealed part of space.

Last season SEAQUEST DSV and LOIS & CLARK

hurt each other's ratings by occupying the same time slot. They are back at it again come Fall. Sadly only one is likely to survive in 1995. NBC and ABC refuse to blink until one knocks off the other.

The real loser will be the audience. Both shows are worth watching.

Sci fi TV currently offers an interesting mix of original programming and spin-offs. STAR TREK lives on in a variety of guises. ROBOCOP and HIGH-LANDER emerged from high profile movie series. LOIS & CLARK and TEK-WAR crossed over from print.

SEAQUEST DSV shows the growing pains of a new idea. THE X-FILES explores new territory for prime time television, and succeeds more than it fails.

SURVIVAL OF THE FITTEST

TIME TRAX died first, the earliest casualty of the new wave. During its second season, fans of the fantastic could choose SEAQUEST, LOIS & CLARK, THE X-

FILES, BABYLON 5, or ROBOCOP. TIME TRAX paled by comparison. The repetitious storylines bored even loyal viewers.

The most interesting series survived. They grow and add change over time. HIGHLANDER, ROBO-COP, SEAQUEST DSV, LOIS & CLARK, BABYLON 5, THE X-FILES, and STAR TREK—DEEP SPACE NINE offer texture and a context to build on.

TEKWAR may not last after it goes weekly in the fall of 1994. More science fiction shows wait in the wings.

Most genres go through cycles on television. It just happens to be science fiction's turn.

The last time this happened was 15 years ago. They were Glen Larsen's big budget disasters. Their failure on network TV still keeps ABC, CBS, and NBC gun-shy of the genre. Nearly all sci-fi series appear in syndication.

THE FUTURE THROUGH THE PAST

Two years from now half of the non-STAR

TREK science fiction series will still be on. Whether this will cause other producers to avoid science fiction is anybody's guess. More channels and more markets bring more need for programming.

The horror series TALES FROM THE CRYPT succeeds on HBO. Showtime plans a revival of THE OUTER LIMITS.

The briefly popular ALIEN NATION ended on a cliffhanger a few years ago. It will now be resolved in a TV movie featuring the original actors. More ALIEN NATION films may follow.

Many possibilities remain. The next new science fiction series on television may prove to be the best ever!

BORING, BUT NECESSARY ORDERING INFORMATION

Payment:

Use our new 800 # and pay with your credit card or send check or money order directly to our address. All payments must be made in U.S. funds and please do not send cash.

Shipping:

We offer several methods of shipment. Sometimes a book can be delayed if we are temporarily out of stock. You should note whether you prefer us to ship the book as soon as available, send you a merchandise credit good for other goodies, or send your money back immediately.

Normal Post Office: $3.75 for the first book and $1.50 for each additional book. These orders are filled as quickly as possible. Shipments normally take 5 to 10 days, but allow up to 12 weeks for delivery.

Special UPS 2 Day Blue Label Service or Priority Mail: Special service is available for desperate Couch Potatoes. These books are shipped within 24 hours of when we receive the order and normally take 2 to 3 three days to get to you. The cost is $10.00 for the first book and $4.00 each additional book .

Overnight Rush Service: $20.00 for the first book and $10.00 each additional book.

U.s. Priority Mail: $6.00 for the first book and $3.00.each additional book.

Canada And Mexico: $5.00 for the first book and $3.00 each additional book.

Foreign: $6.00 for the first book and $3.00 each additional book.

Please list alternatives when available and please state if you would like a refund or for us to backorder an item if it is not in stock.

COUCH POTATO INC.   5715 N. Balsam Rd   Las Vegas, NV 89130   (702)658-2090

Use Your Credit Card 24 HRS — Order toll Free From: **(800)444-2524** Ext 67

ORDER FORM

_____ Trek Crew Book $9.95	_____ Number Six: The Prisoner Book $14.95
_____ Best Of Enterprise Incidents $9.95	_____ Gerry Anderson: Supermarionation $17.95
_____ Trek Fans Handbook $9.95	_____ Addams Family Revealed $14.95
_____ Trek: The Next Generation $14.95	_____ Bloodsucker: Vampires At The Movies $14.95
_____ The Man Who Created Star Trek: $12.95	_____ Dark Shadows Tribute $14.95
_____ 25th Anniversary Trek Tribute $14.95	_____ Monsterland Fear Book $14.95
_____ History Of Trek $14.95	_____ The Films Of Elvis $14.95
_____ The Man Between The Ears $14.95	_____ The Woody Allen Encyclopedia $14.95
_____ Trek: The Making Of The Movies $14.95	_____ Paul Mccartney: 20 Years On His Own $9.95
_____ Trek: The Lost Years $12.95	_____ Yesterday: My Life With The Beatles $14.95
_____ Trek: The Unauthorized Next Generation $14.95	_____ Fab Films Of The Beatles $14.95
_____ New Trek Encyclopedia $19.95	_____ 40 Years At Night: The Tonight Show $14.95
_____ Making A Quantum Leap $14.95	_____ Exposing Northern Exposure $14.95
_____ The Unofficial Tale Of Beauty And The Beast $14.95	_____ The La Lawbook $14.95
_____ Complete Lost In Space $19.95	_____ Cheers: Where Everybody Knows Your Name $14.95
_____ ..doctor Who Encyclopedia: Baker $19.95	_____ SNL! The World Of Saturday Night Live $14.95
_____ Lost In Space Tribute Book $14.95	_____ The Rockford Phile $14.95
_____ Lost In Space With Irwin Allen $14.95	_____ Encyclopedia Of Cartoon Superstars $14.95
_____ Doctor Who: Baker Years $19.95	_____ How To Create Animation $14.95
_____ Doctor Who: Pertwee Years $19.95	_____ How To Draw Art For Comic Books $14.95
_____ Batmania Ii $14.95	_____ King And Barker:an Illustrated Guide $14.95
_____ The Green Hornet $14.95 _____ Special Edition $16.95	_____ King And Barker: An Illustrated Guide II $14.95

100% Satisfaction Guaranteed.

We value your support. You will receive a full refund as long as the copy of the book you are not happy with is received back by us in reasonable condition. No questions asked, except we would like to know how we failed you. Refunds and credits are given as soon as we receive back the item you do not want.

NAME:_____

STREET:_____

CITY:_____

STATE:_____

ZIP:_____

TOTAL:_____ SHIPPING_____

SEND TO: Couch Potato, Inc. 5715 N. Balsam Rd., Las Vegas, NV 89130